"A WILDERNESS STUDY"

Dr Claudette King

A WILDERNESS STUDY

Doctoral: Christian Education

Dr. Claudette King

Dedication

This work is dedicated to Elder Kevin Hutchinson, a good friend, one whom I respect as an oracle of God. Someone who without knowing what God was doing at the time sent me to do a study on the wilderness. At a time in my life when I myself was going through my own wilderness experience, unsure of what was happening God would use him to direct me to study the wilderness. A task I took on, without having any idea or inclination that this study would become my publishable work.

This study aided me in understanding what God was bringing me through and to; and brought about a deep settled peace in my Spirit, enabling me to be more focused in my ministry.

Continue to walk in the Spirit my friend and cease not to speak the word of God.

Thank You..

Contents

Appreciation & Thanks

I acknowledge my husband, John who has been so patient with me, teaching me silently how to be better at everything I do. You are my greatest fan, and I love you. To Nathan and Ronjerome, thanks for bearing with me, when I was snappy and tired, because of late nights and early mornings, working tirelessly to get this done. You are two of the purest people I know, for you have no ulterior motive when you tell me the truth. I love you both.

- To my pastor, Bishop Joseph A. Dawes and his lovely wife, First Lady Yvonne Dawes for support, advice and prayers. I love you both; you are true pillars of faith and sound examples. Keep praying me up.

- To Dr. Gloria Foward and Dr. Sharon Johnson who continued, against all odds, to speak those things which be not as though they were, encouraging me, that GOD will do it! Yes he has, to God be the glory. I am very grateful to Dr. Foward who inspired me to complete my doctoral dissertation, and publish it as a book for world-wide distribution that would minister to the need of his people as they go through their wilderness experience victoriously.

- To Bishop Brooks for his unwavering support and his steadfast belief in not just capturing but holding on to the vision—you are truly a visionary.

Thank you for making a landmark day a reality. I love you and First Lady Brooks for you have been there to listen and to guide with humour (First Lady Brooks) and a stern tone (Bishop Brooks).

- To Elder Trevor Udennis & First Lady Julia Udennis for their advice, encouragement and humour, when everyone else got ruffled by uncontrollable events, Elder Udennis' laugh alone was enough to cheer and calm in many stormy situations, keep on laughing.

- To all my family and friends who have stood by and supported me in hard times, in trying times, in desperate & dark times, praying for me, encouraging me and allowing me to speak to my spirit whilst teaching them the Word. Shirley & Rosie I love you. You are two of my dearest friends.

- To my sister Inez, who gave me the financial and *"slap on the head— big sister"* support (as big sisters do) I love you sis, and hey, hope you are proud of me...

Abstract

There are many references from which we can draw, when we look into the scriptures. Various accounts are recorded of those who had to encounter some kind of wilderness experience. It is not easy or pleasant when we meet upon our hardship, trials, or tests. However, these are to be expected on this Christian journey. James chapter 1 warns us:

Jas 1:2   My brethren, count it all joy when ye fall into divers temptations;

Jas 1:3   Knowing *this*, that the trying of your faith worketh patience. Jas 1:4   But let patience have *her* perfect work, that ye may be perfect and entire, wanting nothing.

Jas 1:5   If any of you lack wisdom, let him ask of God, that giveth to all *men* liberally, and upbraideth not; and it shall be given him.

Brethren, count it all joy *when*: -when signifies, it is going to happen. Had James said "**if**", it would have meant that maybe we could go through some trials, but then maybe not.

However the scripture verse uses the word "WHEN"... therefore we can rest assure that trials, hardship, testing, or we can sum it all up and call it a *Wilderness Experience* must be encountered.

Realistically, we don't rejoice in our tribulations, our wilderness experiences do not invoke joy and rejoicing, instead we are frustrated, angry, bitter, thereby losing precious time and missing what God is doing with us. Often we resort to feelings of depression and have a pity party, while being in turmoil in our minds about what we have done to bring about such an experience. We struggle in our minds, we struggle in our flesh, we struggle in our spirit, all the time ignoring the one thing we should do, which proves usually to be the hardest thing; that is, to approach God in prayer and earnest supplication, and wait for an answer. While God will not always tell us what he is doing with us, he will give us instruction as to what he wants us to do.

When we find ourselves in a wilderness, we will need direction, therefore; we must go to God, for then he will be our compass. We will need provision, therefore, we must go to God, for then he will be our provider. We will need protection, therefore, we must go to God, for then he will be our protector, our shelter from the harsh elements. We must approach God in our wilderness experiences, allowing our flesh to be subjected to our spirit, otherwise, we will continue to struggle, making wrong turns and wrong decisions, whilst wandering in a place, lost; not knowing where to go or how to come out of our wildernesses in the Power of the Spirit, as God intends.

Foreword

I am indeed humbled to have been given the privilege to present the foreword to this magnificent work, "A Wilderness Study", by Dr. Claudette King. This publishable work will inspire the hearts of many to believe God, as they journey to their God-ordained destiny. Jeremiah 29:11 states *"For I know the thoughts that I think towards you saith God, thoughts of peace and not of evil to give you an expected end"*. He created us with purpose and destiny and He is well able to bring us to an expected end with joy, peace, and victory. However, to successfully achieve the plan that God has for us, we must completely yield ourselves to be guided by the Holy Spirit, through obedience to his Word. In other words, the Bible is the road map that will take us from earth, where we face tribulation, economic setbacks, and family breakdown, to our paradisiacal home that God has prepared for us in heaven John (14:1-3).

The scriptures also bear witness that we will personally experience sufferings, sicknesses, deep wounds and hurts and financial disasters. The author of this book elucidates and defines this phase of our lives as our wilderness experience. She has also given us the reason we must journey through these experiences trusting in God. The reader of this book will obtain enlightenment and revelation that God is with them during His process of purification to bring about the necessary changes in our lives to transform us to the image of his Dear Son, Jesus Christ. If we suffer, we shall also reign with him. (II Timothy 2:12, Romans 8:29, I Corinthians 3:18).

This scholarly work by Dr Claudette King, examines the life of various Biblical characters to emphasize that God was with them through their wilderness journey and brought them successfully to their expected end. According to the writer *"This (spiritual) experience does not necessarily come about because of sin or wrong doings, but rather at a time when God is ready to transition you from one place to another; or when He is preparing you for a great work."* She emphasizes that *wilderness experiences allows the "traveller" to get close to God, to understand what is happening and embrace what is about to come.*

As you read the account of Moses, the Children of Israel, David, Job, John the Baptist and Jesus, I am certain that you will find areas of significance and similarity; from which you can draw encouragement, strength, direction, knowledge, and revelation applicable to your own circumstance.

Be blessed as you embark upon understanding more through "A Wilderness Study.

Dr. Gloria J. Foward,
President
International Apostolic University of Grace and Truth, Inc...

Introduction

Deu 8:2   *And thou shalt remember all the way which the LORD thy God led thee these forty years in the wilderness, to humble thee, and to prove thee, to know what was in thine heart, whether thou wouldest keep his commandments, or no.*

Often when we find ourselves in hard or trying times in our lives, we seldom remember key scriptures such as Deuteronomy 8:2. Scriptures that is definitive in its message, showing us that with everything, even the things we find uncomfortable and trying, God has locked purpose concerning us. In Deuteronomy 8:2, God led Israel through the wilderness to:

1. **Humble them:** You might say humble them? But they were slaves who had only come out of bondage, why would they be proud? Remember, all the nations around had heard how God had fought for them, and that had struck fear into their hearts. They could have developed some pride, knowing that they were victorious in battle. Also if we look at 2 Chronicles 7:14, the scripture lends impression that prayer, seeking God's face and turning from wicked ways, are signs of humility. When we consider it; Israel had many times gone after other

gods, they had conformed to the ways and customs of the heathen nations around them, clear signs that they were not seeking God and turning from their wicked ways. No saved individual can approach God without repenting, [*to repent, means to change one's mind*] and we know from reading the scriptures that Israel was warned by numerous prophets to turn back to God, to change their mind from going after other gods and "repent" towards God. God wanted to humble Israel; get them to seek after him, turn from following idols and always go to him first. Therefore, the several trials they faced whilst travelling through the wilderness was to lead them to God.

2.

2. **Prove them:** Prove means to provide evidence of. Israel had numerous occasion to "provide evidence" to God of their intention towards him, showing him that they would trust him, approach him first, rely on him only and communicate with him in everything, and not just before and after a battle. Remember, as a nation, Israel had recently been delivered out of bondage and was being led through the wilderness. God was presenting them with the best opportunity to prove themselves to him. He had taken them out of bondage and made them rich with the wealth of their slave masters, they rejoiced and were joyful giving him thanks, but what did they do when they got to the first obstacle, the Red Sea? They murmured and looked back to their place of bondage. All throughout their journey, it was a constant struggle to get them to provide evidence to God through their faith, that

they trusted him to lead them to their promise, yet they never really did.

3.   **Know what was in their heart:** Have you ever seen a teenager who is being reprimanded, and they stand listening but their body
language is telling you exactly what they think? You know as soon as they walk off, they are going to disregard everything they were told. You can see through their body language and attitude, what is in their heart. God also wanted Israel to know what was in their heart. God already knew, he had told Abraham over four hundred years prior what would become of his people, Israel. God wanted Israel to know that their heart was not panting after him. God knew they would not keep his commandments, another prophecy he gave to Moses.

> a.   whether they would keep his commandments or not—we see in Deuteronomy chapter 31, God told Moses what would become of Israel and instructed Moses to write the experiences from Egypt to where they were and even what would happen when they entered the Promised Land, and that song, was written by Moses for a testimony against Israel.

Now one thing I always hold to is not to let people become prophets [especially when that prophecy is not a good thing] over my life. I will strive to prove them wrong. You would think then that since Moses had written that Israel would go after other gods, that Israel would use it as a warning of things not to do, but no, God had spoken the words, not as a prophecy over Israel, but more out of knowing what the heart of Israel would be swayed by, and he knew after all that he had done for them, he did not have first place in their hearts.

I pray today, that after or while reading, you will place God at the highest place in your heart. Hold nothing before or higher than God, for it is he who is able to love you unconditionally, even whilst knowing your flaws and it is he who will take you through the wilderness to (1) humble you, get you to draw closer to him, (2) prove you, so that you can provide him with evidence that you trust him to take you through, and (3) to know what is in your heart. For everything that we do with or for God requires our heart. Our hearts *must* be engaged and fixed toward God; even in our wildernesses – especially in our wildernesses.

CHAPTER 1

"What is a Wilderness Experience?"

A wilderness experience is one that you will often have to travel alone. One where the terrain, natural or spiritual; will demand all of what you have. Even if you started out on the journey running, by the time you are well into the wilderness, you will be drained, you will be tired, you will be weary, you will need to pull out strength from the inner recesses of your Spirit.

A fitting Scripture is:

> *2Co 12:10*   *Therefore I take pleasure in infirmities, in reproaches, in necessities, in persecutions, in distresses for Christ's sake:* ***for when I am weak, then am I strong***.

A wilderness experience will require you to pull out what you have in you. For in a wilderness there is no food, or water or

sustenance coming from anywhere. All the elements are requiring of and taking from you, not giving to you. The heat of the wilderness will require you to be hydrated enough to endure the journey. The cold of the wilderness in the night will

require you to have an inner fire (the Holy Ghost) that will keep you warm. The deadly animals that can cause your demise will require you to be on your guard, watching always, praying without ceasing. For losing focus could cost you your life. The dry arid terrain will require you to sustain yourself, for there is no food with which you can be sustained or replenished. So you will have to have enough bread (the Word) in you to keep you throughout the duration of the journey.

Everything you have in you will have to be used to sustain you, spiritually, physically and emotionally. For otherwise, you could lose hope and give up; allowing the elements or the creatures or the terrain to get the better of you. You could lose strength, becoming so weak that you cannot take another step or you could lose your spirit and give up on God. But the devil is a liar, for God is not unfaithful, he will not allow you to be tempted above that which you are able to bear. He will with the temptation, make a way of escape that you will be able to bear it.

> *1Co 10:13*　　*There hath no temptation taken you but such as is common to man: but God is faithful, who will not suffer you to be tempted above that ye are able; but will with the temptation also make a way to escape, that ye may be able to bear it.*

Just as God did for Hagar, he can create an oasis in the middle of the desert to re-hydrate your spirit. Like he did for David, he can lay you beside still waters and restore your soul. Just like he did for the children of Israel, he can prepare a smorgasbord (a dish of various food) for you in the middle of a wilderness without the aid of a chef. Just as he did for John the Baptist, he can keep you on what you have available to you and just like Jesus, when he takes you into the wilderness, it is by the Spirit, it is in his will, it is only for you to be tempted, but not defeated, for though he has led you to be tempted, he has made a way of escape . . . look for the escape that God has made for you, that is the God we serve. Whatever wilderness you may be facing, I have one word for you, **ENDURE**

Jeremiah 26:14

As for me, behold, I am in your hand:
do with me as seemeth good and meet
unto you.

CHAPTER 2

"Why Go through a Wilderness?"

The word "wilderness" refers to a wild rough land, a wasteland or backwoods. Somewhere usually uninhabited and left uncultivated, sometimes deliberately (like a forest or mountainous region). Wildernesses are remote outdoor places, areas that are empty or barren, which could have a dry, arid, rocky or sandy terrain. It could also be somewhere that is water logged, with rough trees, shrubs or bushes. Whatever the terrain, it is usually somewhere deserted and uninhabited. This is the natural wilderness, an isolated place with harsh and unpleasant terrain.

A (spiritual) wilderness usually lends a feeling of isolation, it causes the one journeying to feel deserted and lonely. It is a (spiritual) place where your prayers seem to go unanswered, and if you are not careful, you will stop praying. It causes your spirit to become drained, as you are depending on all that you have in you to carry you through.

This (spiritual) experience does not necessarily come about

because of sin or wrong doings, but rather at a time when God is ready to transition you from one place to another or when He is preparing you for a great work. A wilderness experience could also come about with a loss of power or influence. After having been in a position of authority or leadership, should that change, then; that state of being without the position of authority or leadership could be described as a Positional wilderness experience.

Wilderness experiences are often embarked upon alone, as it allows the "traveler" space, time and opportunity to get close to God, to know more about God, to understand what is happening and embrace what is about to come. This is however, dependent on how the "traveler" views the experience, or how they react to what is happening at that time. It could be easier to throw in the towel, or simply give up, thinking God has allowed or done you a grave injustice. The "traveler" could become resentful or bitter, whilst misreading the signals or the will of God. For it is not God's will that any should perish, especially not in a wilderness, like the children of Israel. God will take you to your promise, the question is, will you through fear and inexperience in warfare, allow your perception of your enemies to cause you not to enter your promise. For in a wilderness, a lot depends on your perception, what do you see. Yes, you are in a wilderness, but what do you see . . . ? For if you can only see the reason (you think) you are going through that experience and you focus on that reason, then you will most definitely miss what God is doing. For the reason God led the Children of Israel through the wilderness, was not because Egypt had cornered them in battle, it was not that Moses had taken a wrong turn, but rather, God had decided to lead them away from the Philistines land. This was because the children of Israel were slaves, not accustomed to seeing war and God knew they would not have been able (because of their perception) to take the route through the Philistines land.

> Exo 13:17   And it came to pass, when Pharaoh had let the people go, that God led them not through the way of the land of the Philistines, although that was near; for God said, Lest peradventure the people repent when they see war, and they return to Egypt:

Therefore, when you are going through a wilderness, your sight has to be clear, your sight, both physical and spiritual needs to be clear and focused on looking for the way of escape which God has made.

When going through a wilderness experience, it will not be an enjoyable time in your walk with God. It will be a time of great uncertainty, pain, hurt, and even doubt. You will feel alone, isolated, forsaken and destitute. It will be hard to pray, hard to fast, you will have to push through feelings of loneliness and seclusion, feelings of giving up and throwing in the towel, feelings of weakness and spiritual impoverishment. When you are spiritually drained, spiritually tired, spiritually weak and can almost touch the invisible canopy over your head, seemingly blocking your prayers and cries for help, you must push and reach into your store house of praise and worship, to do whatever it takes to keep on going, for truly, you will reap, if you do not faint.

Isaiah 55:6 states, "seek ye the LORD while he may be found, call ye upon him while he is near". This scripture should be obeyed before you get to your wilderness experience. For it is a precaution to all of us as saints of God to seek God while we are not in our wildernesses, and stay close to God when things are spiritually good. Store up your prayers, store up your praises, store up your fasting, store up your Bible studies, for there is surely coming a wilderness experience, where you will not have the physical or spiritual strength to fast, or to pray. You won't feel like worshipping, or praising. Your spiritual deposits made during times of great rejoicing and on your mountain tops, will be necessary; as these will become withdrawals of strength. Your spiritual energy will have to be expended wisely, as during your wilderness experience you won't find anything that will be as sustenance to you, so all that you had deposited, will need to be enough to keep you and see you through the experience.

I am reminded of something a friend shared with me at a time when I had just started on my wilderness experience. Without knowing what was going on with me at the time, someone over four thousand miles away, across the ocean, just sent me some information, as we say—"out of the blue". As I lay on my bed, contemplating what I had done wrong, or where I had gone wrong, I opened my email and found a word from God that not only blessed me, but kept me for weeks. It told a story of the eagle.

[1]*The Rebirth of the Eagle*

The eagle has the longest life span of its species, it can live for up to seventy years, but to reach this age, the eagle has to make a hard decision. In its forties, its long and flexible talons, can no longer grab prey which serves as food. Its long and sharp beak becomes bent, its old aged and heavy wings, due to their thick feathers, become stuck to its chest and makes it difficult to fly. The eagle is then left with only two options: option 1: die, option 2: go through a painful process of change, which lasts approximately one hundred and fifty (150) days.

The process requires that the eagle flies to a mountain top and

sit on its nest. There the eagle knocks its beak against a rock until it plucks it out After plucking it out, the eagle will wait for a new beak to grow back and then it proceeds to pluck its talons out.

When its new talons grow back, the eagle starts plucking its old

---

[1] Adaptation from The Rebirth of the Eagle by Mike: ruppi_scifi@yahoo.de

aged feathers. And after five months, the eagle takes its famous flight of rebirth and lives for a further thirty years.

After reading this remarkable story of what the eagle goes through, the scripture in Isaiah 40:29-31 then made much more sense. For the eagle gets to a place where it has to make a decision, it realises that the transition is necessary in order for it to survive.

For not being able to catch prey, would inadvertently cause it to suffer from starvation. Therefore, to avoid dying of hunger, a decision has to be made. Does it sit there and starve to death, or does it go through the metamorphosis necessary to extend its life and make it even more agile, for another three decades?

Like the eagle, we too will arrive at a place where we also have to decide whether to live or die (spiritually). The decision we make, will often cause us to embark upon a wilderness experience, an experience necessary for our spiritual survival. However, we can take heart and find encouragement in the Word of God

Isa 40:29   He giveth power to the faint; and to them that have no might he increaseth strength.

Isa 40:30   Even the youths shall faint and be weary, and the young men shall utterly fall:

Isa 40:31   But they that wait upon the LORD shall renew their strength; they shall

> mount up with wings as eagles; they
> shall run, and not be weary; and they
> shall walk, and not faint.

The mounting up with wings as eagles, refers to the renewing, the rebirth of the eagle. Note therefore, that prior to the mounting up, one suffers from weariness, borders on fainting and has no might. The Word shows that even those who are agile and seemingly strong shall faint and even utterly fall.

Similar to the eagle beating its own beak upon the rock, making it loose in order to tear it out so that a new beak can reform and plucking out its talons one by one is the removing of old things, old hurts, old pains, old thoughts, traditional thinking and ways, removing the weight and the things which so easily beset us. How painful that must be, but the eagle knows it is necessary for its survival, for his old talons can no long grab and tear prey, allowing him to gain strength from feeding himself therefore it's not effective and whatever is not effective, or fulfilling its purpose, requires change. Change is needful for purpose to be accomplished.

Imagine the tearing out of its feathers, rendering itself unable to fly. Please note, the eagle could not go through this process on the lowlands, for then he would become prey to other creatures. It is therefore imperative for it to be on the mountain top and away from impending danger from other animals prior to embarking upon this transition. So it is with us as saints of God, we must get to a place in God where we recognize the call of God to a place of change, the need for transition and be sensitive to the leading of the Spirit in answering the call. This takes a mountain top experience with God.

We can say therefore, that a wilderness experience is like a "sandwich" of events. This terminology is borrowed from what is known as a "sandwich feedback", where an individual will give a number of sentences, but laid out in a particular way so as to bring encouragement to the hearer. They would deliver a good statement, then a not so good one, then follow that up with a good one. Much like the "sandwich feedback approach" the wilderness experience is made up of a sandwich of events.

1. Having a mountain top experience, where we recognize the need for change
2. The wilderness experience where we heed the change and then;
3. The soaring to even higher heights experience; after we have gone through the change.

It is safe to say that without the mountain top experience; God will not be able to translate to your spirit the necessity of the change. In order for us as human beings, or mankind to recognize where we are, God needs to be able to speak to our hearts, which means, he may send someone to preach a word that pricks and causes us to recognize where we are. A friend may be moved to speak to us on a level that only they can, but our hearts must be so humble that we are in a place to take harsh but truthfully needed critique. God could send a number of people to try us in the same area, until we recognize, the problem may just be "me" and not everyone else, thereby embracing the change that is about to begin in our hearts.

Unfortunately, not everyone will allow for, or embrace changes. Some of us will never accept that we are the problem and not part of the solution, some of us will never admit that we have an area or areas of our lives, personality, character, belief system or ways that needs to be changed. However, for those who do, when we do, we open up to the move of God and allow him to bring about a great transformation in us. It reminds me of the scripture from Paul in Galatians 4:19, My little children of whom I travail in birth again until Christ be formed in you. There must be a continuous transformation - until, inferring to a time when the transformation shall be complete - Christ, the anointed one, be formed, a completion of the metamorphosis has taken place, the ultimate formation of Christ Jesus in us.

Hence, the reason for us going through a wilderness or several wilderness experiences is for the complete formation of Christ in us. Everything seems to be going well in your walk with God, you have the testimony that all is fine and you are truly happy, you are hearing from God, reading the Word and praying. If this is the case then, you are about to embark upon a wilderness experience, soon.

1. Start listening for the voice of God when you pray and record what he is saying to you.

2.   After a while, things that you usually don't pay attention to will begin to aggravate you.

3.   You want to see more done.

4.   You grow impatient with where you are.

5.   You can't understand why no one else is bothered about the things you are bothered about.

6.   You feel like you are the only one who sees the things you see in the spirit.

Prepare yourself, God is about to take you higher. For you are exhibiting signs of maturity beyond the level you are at and it is time for change.

Questions for Chapter 2:

Here are a number of questions to aid you in your research.
Think about the last wilderness experience you went through, detail
the signs of God preparing you for the experience.

1. Make a note of your "sandwich experience", i.e. - a mountain
   top period followed by a wilderness experience followed by
   the soar to new things/place/heights.
2. If there was no "soaring" to new things/ place /heights in God,
   then did you obey God whilst in the wilderness?
   a. If yes, give details of the obedience
   b. If no, give details and reason for the disobedience and
      the consequence of that disobedience
3. Identify someone in the scriptures that had a similar
   wilderness experience to yours, give reasons for your answer
4. Compare and contrast how they came out of the wilderness
   as opposed to how you came out of the wilderness
5. Would you do anything different, the next time around, give
   reasons for your answer?

Psalms 119:105

*Thy word is a lamp unto my feet, and a light
unto my path*

CHAPTER 3

"A Wilderness Study Reference"

Definition

Before I look at people in the scriptures who have gone through some kind of wilderness experience, I have extracted from the Strong's Exhaustive Concordance, the Hebrew and Greek meaning of "wilderness" and have detailed the number of occurrences in the scripture as a reference guide.

Wilderness (According to the Vine's Expository Dictionary)

Wilderness according to the Vine's
Expository Dictionary:

1. [2]**EREMIA**: *(an uninhabited place)*, is translated

---

[2] Vine's Expository Dictionary

"wilderness" in the A.V. of Matthew 15:33 and Mark 8:4 (R.V., "a desert place") in R.V., and A.V., "wilderness" in 2 Corinthians 11:26. SEE DESERT, A.V.,

(in the Sept., Is 60:20; Ezekiel35:4,9)

2.   [3]**EREMOS**: an adjective signifying desolate, deserted, lonely, is used as a noun, and rendered "wilderness" 32 times in the A.V. in Matthew 24:26 and John 6:31, R.V., "wilderness" (A.V. "desert").

For the R.V., "deserts" in Luke 5:16 and 8:29

Strong's # Meaning

There are several meanings in the Strong's dictionary for the word "wilderness". They are listed below. (For the respective Bible verses please see the Appendix) Please note: Strong's style of referencing is quite exhaustive, as they have referenced by number, every Hebrew (H—Old Testament) or Greek (G—New Testament) word with the English meaning.

The Numbering System Explained

The numbers are as follows: e.g. 4057 is the Strong's number for wilderness. The underlined number, starting with a letter (H or G, where H is for Hebrew and G is for Greek, (as the Old Testament is written in Hebrew, whilst the

---

[3] Vine's Expository Dictionary

New Testament was originally written in Greek) is a number which translates to wilderness also. This may be similar in meaning to the first referenced number. Please be reminded, that if you have found the word "wilderness" in the Old Testament, the reference will be accompanied by the letter H and for the New Testament, the reference letter accompanying is G.

[4]**4057**: midbâr - mid-bawr': From *H1696* (**H1696 -** dâbar daw-bar': A primitive root; perhaps properly to arrange; but used figuratively (of words) to speak; rarely (in a destructive sense) to subdue: - answer, appoint, bid, command, commune, declare, destroy, give, name, promise, pronounce, rehearse, say, speak, be spokesman, subdue, talk, teach, tell, think, use [entreaties], utter, X well, X work) .in the sense of driving; a pasture (that is, open field, whither cattle are driven); by implication a desert; also speech (including its organs): - desert, south, speech, wilderness.

[5]**8414**: tôhû - to'-hoo: From an unused root meaning to lie waste; a desolation (of surface), that is, desert; figuratively a worthless thing; adverbially in vain: - confusion, empty place, without form, nothing, (thing of) nought, vain, vanity, waste, wilderness.

---

[4] The New Exhaustive Strong's Concordance of the Bible
[5] The New Strong's Exhaustive Concordance of the Bible

[6]**6160**: 'ărâbâh—ar-aw-baw': From *H6150* (**H6150 -** 'ârab - aw-rab': A primitive root (rather identical with *H6148* through the idea of covering with a texture); to grow dusky at sundown: - be darkened, (toward) evening.) (in the sense of sterility); a desert; especially (with the article prefixed) the (generally) sterile valley of the Jordan and its continuation to the Red Sea: - Arabah, champaign, desert, evening, heaven, plain, wilderness. See also *H1026*. (bêyth hâ'ărâbâh - bayth haw-ar-aw-baw' : From *H1004* and *H6160* with the article interposed; house of the Desert; Beth-ha-Arabah, a place in Palestine: - Beth-arabah.)

> [7]**6723**:'othnîy—oth-nee': From an unused root meaning to force; forcible; Othni, an Israelite: - Othni.

> [8]**3452**:yᵉshîymôn—yesh-ee-mone': From *H3456*;(yâsham—yaw-sham': A primitive root; to lie waste: - be desolate.) a desolation:- desert, Jeshimon, solitary, wilderness.

> [9]**6728**: tsîyîy - tsee-ee': From the same as *H6723*;
> ('othnîy - oth-nee': From an unused root meaning to force; forcible; Othni, an Israelite: - Othni.) a desert dweller, that is, nomad or wild beast: - wild beast of the desert, that dwell in (inhabiting) the wilderness.

---

[6] The New Strong's Exhaustive Concordance of the Bible
[7] The New Strong's Exhaustive Concordance of the Bible
[8] The New Strong's Exhaustive Concordance of the Bible
[9] The New Strong's Exhaustive Concordance of the Bible

[10]**6166**: 'ărâd - ar-awd': From an unused root meaning to sequester itself; fugitive; Arad, the name of a place near Palestine, also of a Canaanite and an Israelite: - Arad.

[11]**2048**: hâthal - haw-thal': A primitive root; to deride; by implication to cheat: - deal deceitfully, deceive, mock.

[12]**2047**: hăthâk - hath-awk': Probably of foreign origin; Hathak, a Persian eunuch: - Hatach.

Bible Books Pertaining to Wilderness

Of the 66 books in the Bible, 30 do not mention the word "wilderness". These, when broken down, result in 18 of the 27 New Testament books, and only 12 of the 39 Old Testament books. They are:

1. **Old Testament Books** (which does not contain the word wilderness) Ruth, Ezra, Esther, Ecclesiastes, Daniel, Obadiah, Jonah, Micah, Nahum, Habakkuk, Haggai & Zechariah,

2. **New Testament Books** (which does not contain the word wilderness) Romans, Galatians,

---

[10] The New Strong's Exhaustive Concordance of the Bible
[11] The New Strong's Exhaustive Concordance of the Bible
[12] The New Strong's Exhaustive Concordance of the Bible

Ephesians, Philippians, Colossians, 1 & 2
Thessalonians, 1 & 2 Timothy, Titus, Philemon,
James, 1 & 2 Peter, 1,2 & 3 John & Jude.

You'll find then that more than half (36 in all) of the Bible books carry the word wilderness. Wilderness experiences seem inevitable; for every one of us at some point will encounter "A Wilderness Experience".

Questions for Chapter 3:

In relation to the study notes above *(please see the appendix for the related verses)* choose four scriptures on wilderness, two from the Old Testament and two from the New Testament. Provide explanation on each. Each explanation should be at least one A4 page long.

Psalms 40:2

He brought me up also out of an horrible pit, out of the miry clay, and set my feet upon a rock, and established my goings

CHAPTER 4

"Wildernesses Mentioned"

The wildernesses mentioned in the Bible amounts to twenty-three. They are listed with their meanings displayed:

	Wilderness	Meaning		Wilderness	Meaning
1	Beersheba	Of the oath	13	Judah	Let him (God) be praised
2	Sinai (Sina)	Mountain (same as Horeb) where the Law was given	14	Ziph	Refining place
3	Paran	A wilderness region in the Sinaitic peninsula	15	Maon	Abode
4	The Red Sea	Sea of reeds	16	Engedi	Fountain of a kid
5	Shur	Fortification	17	Gibeon	Hill town
6	Sin	Disobedience of God's law	18	Damascu	Chief city of Aram
7	Zin	Low land	19	Edom	Red
8	Etham	Sea bound	20	Jeruel	Founded by God
9	Moab	Seed	21	Tekoa	Firm, settlement
10	Kedemoth	Ancient places	22	Kadesh	Holy
11	Lebanon	Mountain range (10,000ft) in north Canaan	23	"Egypt"	Black
12	Bethaven	House of nothingness or vanity			

Following, is a look through the lives of some of the wilderness experiences from the scriptures. I have chosen six to study. This is not an extensive list of all those in the scriptures who had such an experience, nor am I saying that only the ones that have been mentioned are the only type of wilderness experiences that exists. But rather, an analysis of those whom I have chosen; to investigate:

1. How the experience came about
2. Where they were in their lives when the need for change became necessary
3. The actual experience they underwent
4. The outcome, after the experience

It is also imperative to note, not all those who experienced a wilderness experience came out of it ready to soar to new heights. However, that we may learn from what they went through, so that we can:

a. Recognise the need for change
b. Be aware when the transition is upon us
c. Know what to expect whilst going through the experience
d. Take courage knowing, we shall reap if we endure
e. Learn from their mistakes so that we can walk out of the experience ready to do exploits for God.

Come with me on this journey as we examine the experiences that some of those mentioned in the Bible went through. 1 Corinthians 10:11 says: "Now all these things happened unto them for ensamples: and they are written for our admonition, upon whom the ends of the world are come." Everything is written that we may learn from them. The good times, the bad times, the great and joyous occasions, the regrettable and sad occasion. God in his wisdom has shown us that the prophets, priests and forefathers of the scriptures were just like us. They had the same experiences, made grave mistakes from which we can draw, realising that like them, we too can go through; for

God has given us his inspired word, profitable for doctrine, reproof, correction, instruction in righteousness, so that by them, we too can be found perfect, thoroughly furnished, unto all good works.

> 2Ti 3:16   All scripture is given by inspiration of God, and is profitable for doctrine, for reproof, for correction, for instruction in righteousness:
>
> 2Ti 3:17   That the man of God may be perfect, thoroughly furnished unto all good works.

Some Wilderness Experiences

Those whom I have chosen to investigate for this work are listed below. I have also included the meaning of their names.

1. Moses: "drawn from the water"
2. The Children of 'Israel'   "God Strives"
3. David   "well beloved"
4. Job   "returning"
5. The Baptist, 'John'   "Jehovah has been gracious"
6. Jesus   "Y' Shu'ah—Jeshua / Jehovah is Salvation"

Questions for Chapter 4:

Choose one other person, not already investigated in this write up, who went through a wilderness experience, and detail the following about their life:

      I.   How the experience came about

     II.   Where they were in their lives when the need for change became necessary

   III. The actual experience they underwent

   IV. The outcome, after the experience

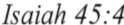

Isaiah 45:4

*For Jacob my servants' sake, and Israel mine elect, I have
even called thee by name: I have surnamed thee, though
thou hast not known me*

CHAPTER 5

"Wilderness Experiences—Moses"

[13]*Moses - H4872,-* הֹשֶׁ

Mosheh mo-sheh'- From *H4871*; drawing out (of the water),
that is, rescued; Mosheh, the Israelitish lawgiver: - Moses.

The chart below shows the birth approximation date for Moses along
with three, forty year span of his life, the corresponding scripture and
the Pharaoh who ruled at each period in time.

[14]

Ex 2:1-10	Acts 7:23-24	Acts 7:29-30	1 Ki 6:1	Num 32:13	Deu 34:7
Found by Pharaoh's daughter	Moses kills the Egyptian	40 Years spent in Midian Pharaoh dies (Ex 2:23)	Leads Exodus from Egypt	40 Years spent in the wilderness	Dies in Moab
Tutmoses I (had no son's, only a daughter)	Hatshepsut Tutmoses II	Tutmoses III	Tutmoses IV (not first born)	Akhenaten (changes religion)	

---

[13] Strong's Exhaustive Concordance of the Bible

[14] http://biblelight.net/moses.htm

History - How Israel Became Slaves in Egypt

Moses, the youngest of three children by Jocebed and her husband Amram, who were both of the tribe of Levi, had an older brother, named Aaron and a sister called Miriam. Moses, born (1525bc), at a period in time where the ruling Pharaoh (Tutmoses 1) had growing concerns about the fast increasing and ever growing number of the Israelites who were enslaved in Egypt.

The Israelites (or Hebrews) had not started out as slaves in Egypt but as free men. They were enslaved when the Bible records that another Pharaoh arose who knew not Joseph. Who was Joseph? Joseph, son of Rachel and Jacob, (whose name God later changed to Israel), was seemingly favoured by his father Jacob. Joseph was the son of his beloved wife, Rachel, who for many years seemed unable to bear children. Joseph was also gifted to dream, and to interpret the dreams he had. His dreams often told of greatness in his future and his impending ruler-ship over his brethren and parents. Hated of his brothers for being his father's favourite and for dreaming of future power and position, they conspired to get rid of him.

Joseph was eventually cast into a pit by his brothers (Gen 37:24) after they originally thought of killing him, but Rueben, an older sibling, intervened in a bid to save his life, hoping to later free him from the pit when the rest of the brothers were not around. However, unknown to him (Reuben) the brothers decided to profit from Joseph's head and so they pulled him up from the pit and sold him to a company of Ishmeelites on their way to Egypt (Gen 37:26-29). These Ishmeelites in turn sold Joseph to Potiphar when they got to Egypt. Joseph however, had risen to the rank of being head of Potiphar's house and through his God-given dreams and gift of interpretation, later became ruler over all the land of Egypt, second only in command to the Pharaoh himself. Why? Why was it possible for a Hebrew slave to attain to such height in a foreign land, away from his brethren and his parents, whom he loved? The answer is because God was with him and everything Joseph did, God prospered (Gen 39:3).

Later on when a famine arose in all the land, Joseph's brothers had to seek for food. This search brought them to Egypt, because Egypt was the only place that seemed to have food. This was because after interpreting Pharaoh's dream, Joseph had been promoted with the task of overseeing the gathering of the grain in the seven years of plenty and storing up for the seven years of famine, according to the dream which God allowed Pharaoh to dream; the interpretation of which God revealed only to Joseph. For his gift of dreams and interpretation would bring him before Kings and allowed him to move into the ordained plan of God. God sent Joseph to Egypt before his brethren to allow his family to be saved and well cared for in a time of famine. What a mighty God we serve.

When Joseph's brothers arrived in Egypt Joseph immediately recognised them, but they not knowing what had become of him, and not expecting to maybe even see him again, let alone seeing him in such a lofty position did not recognise him. Also, Joseph would have reflected his position and prominence in Egypt, rendering him unrecognisable to his brothers, as the customary dress of the Egyptians was quite different to that of the Hebrews.

In time and when Joseph was ready, he revealed himself to his brothers and seeing there was enough food in Egypt, and their brother Joseph was in a place of prominence, they accepted his offer to move to Egypt. Pharaoh had much respect and love for Joseph, and so when Joseph made request for a place for his family, Pharaoh gave him Goshen.

Jacob and his children (as Rachel had now died) settled with their long lost brother and his sons (Ephraim and Manasseh) in Goshen around 1876, approximately seventy-one years later Joseph died in 1805. Roughly about one hundred and forty-six years after Jacob and his family had moved to Egypt and some seventy-five years after Joseph's death, the scripture records in Exodus 1:8 that another king arose in Egypt that did not know Joseph. Seeing that the Hebrews had multiplied to great numbers, more than the Egyptians in their own land, Pharaoh decided to enslave them. Thus the Israelites or Hebrews were made slaves as Pharaoh placed over them tasks masters who whipped them and forced them to work, building cities for Pharaoh.

Moses: Slave or Prince of Egypt

Moses was born to parents who were slaves in Egypt, his brother and sister were probably already working for the

29

Egyptians. They were accustomed to a life of being told what to do, when they could eat, a life where they were prisoners.

Moses on the other hand, because he had been rescued from the water by Pharaoh's daughter, and was given the privilege to be raised in the luxury of Egypt; he was used to fine things. Moses did not know a life of slavery, apart from what he saw the Hebrews going through. He was schooled among the best in Egypt and was being groomed to be the next king over Egypt.

[15]Historian Egyptologist records (if we refer to the table which was seen earlier) that the custom of Egypt was such; because Pharaoh (Tutmose 1) had no son, his daughter, Nefure would be next in line to be pharaoh. However, when she claimed Moses as her son, he became the rightful heir and would rule by her side, until he was old enough to rule the kingdom. It is recorded that Nefure's father, the Pharaoh (Tutmose 1) died when she was about fifteen years old.

Because Moses was being groomed for the throne, he was schooled in all the wisdom of Egypt, and it was expected of him to take his place by the side of "his mother" who raised him (Neferu-ra), the statues and hieroglyphics reflected this. It was the custom in Egypt that a prince of Egypt; someone who would later rule, wears one lock of hair on the right side, as a child. This can be seen in the depiction of the following statues. It is believed that the statue is of Neferu-ra and the infant Moses. A prince of Egypt would

---

[15] http://biblelight.net/moses.htm

also be depicted wearing the serpent on its forehead as seen in the statues.

 As Moses grew to adulthood, he assumed the title of Tutmoses II (Senmut), as heir to the throne of Egypt.

Hebrews 11:24-26 records

Heb 11:24   By faith Moses, when he was come to years, refused to be called the son of Pharaoh's daughter;

Heb 11:25   Choosing rather to suffer affliction with the people of God, than to enjoy the pleasures of sin for a season;

Heb 11:26   Esteeming the reproach of Christ greater riches than the treasures in Egypt: for he had respect unto the recompense of the reward.

16

Moses Born	Moses 40	Acts 7:29-30
1525 B.C.—Ex 2:1-10	1485 B.C.—Acts 7:23-24	**Moses 40 Years spent in Midian** Pharaoh dies (Ex 2:23)
Moses found by Pharaoh's daughter in the Nile in Memphis (Ex 2:5-9) Moses named by Princess Nefure (Hatshepsut) (Ex 2:10). "Senmut" is another Egyptian name given to Moses when he came to live at the palace. At Deir El Bahri, there is a wall which depicts the birth of the future heir to the throne, one scene shows a baby boy in the arms of Hatshepsut–the infant Moses!	**Moses kills the Egyptian** The last that we hear of Senenmut (Moses) is in year 16 of Hatshepsut's reign. Moses when 40 years old slays an Egyptian (Ex 2:12) and flees Egypt (Ex 2:15) because pharaoh (Moses replacement) wanted to kill him. Tomb No. 71 at Deir El Bahri was first of two tombs intended for Moses (Senenmut). Tomb No. 353 was the second, but work stopped when he fled Egypt, and the tomb remains unfinished.	
Tutmoses I had no sons, only a daughter This is the pharaoh who issued the decree that all the infant sons born to the Israelites were to be thrown into the river Nile, but that infant girls were permitted to live. (Exodus 1:22) The third king of the 18th Dynasty Tutmoses I was a commoner by birth. He had married Ahmose, a sister of Amenhotep I, and was named king when the king died childless. Tutmoses I had no sons, but was the father of Nefure (Hatshepsut), the princess who is the most likely candidate for having found Moses in the Nile. First Pharaoh buried in the Valley of the Kings.	**Hatshepsut—Tutmoses II Senmut/Tutmoses II** (Moses) is groomed to become pharaoh. He is the architect of Deir El Bahri, the mortuary temple of Hatshepsut. Daughter of Tutmoses I. It is thought she was about age fifteen when her father died. Hatshepsut married her half-brother, Thutmose II, who had a son, Thutmose III, by a concubine/minor wife (Mutnofret). Co-ruled with Tutmoses III who was only a child when Tutmoses II died. Tutmoses III was the illegitimate son of Tutmoses II (not a son of Hatshepsut). In 1488, six years prior to her death, all official records of Hatshepsut ceased.	**Tutmoses III** Assumed the position of Pharoah with the demise of Hatshepsut. (Moses was his competitor for the position of pharaoh). Tutmoses III was "The Napoleon of ancient Egypt and captured over 350 cities.

---

[16] http://biblelight.net/moses.htm

Moses, as I mentioned before would have been groomed with a hope of someday being king over Egypt. Yet Moses refused what Egypt had to offer. This must have been a blow for Queen Hatshepsut, as she had given Moses the best of what Egypt had to offer. Saving his life from certain death and claiming him, a Hebrew slave as her son. Grooming him in the wisdom and affairs of kingly preparation, she thought for sure, he would have chosen to rule beside her. How betrayed she must have felt when Moses sided with the Hebrews, deciding to suffer affliction with the people of God, rather than enjoying the pleasures of sin for a season. Verse 26 stated that Moses esteemed the reproach of Christ greater riches than the treasures in Egypt. Moses must have had the opportunity to make a decision. He had to decide between the riches and treasure of Egypt or the fate of being returned to his native tribe and becoming a slave. It is thought that the scripture in Exodus 2:11 was an act of rebellion on Moses part, to show what his choice had been.

Exo 2:11   *And it came to pass in those days, when Moses was grown, that he went out unto his brethren, and looked on their burdens: and he spied an Egyptian smiting an Hebrew, one of his brethren.*

His going out unto his brethren to look on their burdens, signifies that Moses had already identified himself with the Hebrews. How did Moses know them to be his brethren,

[17]either by divine revelation, or by conversing with his nurse, who was his mother; who, doubtless, instructed him while he was with her, as far as he was capable of being informed of things, by which means he became apprised that he was an Hebrew and not an Egyptian, though he was known as the son of Pharaoh's daughter, which he refused to be called when he knew his parentage, and linage. Being schooled by his nurse, (his birth-mother), she had taught him that he was Hebrew, she had taught him the way and the laws of God. She had taught him about the God of Abraham, the God of Isaac and the God of Jacob. This would have been a fascinating thing for Moses to hear and be drawn to, as the idol gods of Egypt (which were so many) had not done anything to which he could compare what his birth mother was teaching him concerning this God of the Hebrews. Now he went out from Pharaoh's palace, which in a short time he entirely relinquished, to visit his brethren, and converse with them, to understand their case and circumstances: which they were obliged to carry, and were very heavy, and with which they were pressed; he looked at them with grief and concern, and considered in his mind how to relieve them, if possible: Remember also, God had chosen Moses from birth, having him saved by the daughter of the very man who had declared the judgment and passed death upon the sons of the Hebrews, God saved Moses from the wrath and decree of the time. Satan

---

[17] http://biblelight.net/moses.htm

would have targeted Moses, for surely giving up the treasures of Egypt would have been something Moses would have had to ponder over and maybe even struggle with. It would not have been easy; Moses would have had to make a hard choice. Taking it upon himself to execute judgment in the killing of the Egyptian for doing his job, this act

Exo 2:11   *And it came to pass in those days, when Moses was grown, that he went out unto his brethren, and looked on their burdens: and he spied an Egyptian smiting an Hebrew,   one of his brethren.*

Exo 2:12   *And he looked this way and that way, and when he saw that there was no man, he slew the Egyptian, and hid him in the sand.*

of murder would start Moses on a trail that would lead him to seeking and finding the God whom his mother Jocebed, his nurse had secretly taught him about.

After realising that the deed he had committed had been found out, that is; the killing of the Egyptian, Moses fled in a bid

Exo 2:14   And he said, Who made thee a prince and a judge over us? intendest thou to kill me, as thou killedst the Egyptian? And Moses feared, and said, Surely this thing is known.

save his life from certain death. For the Pharaoh at that time would have taken the liberty of using this crime to kill him, seeing he was the rival of Moses and seemingly did not like either Hatshepsut or Moses.

Exo 2:15   Now when Pharaoh heard this thing, he sought to slay Moses. But Moses fled from the face of Pharaoh, and dwelt in the land of Midian: and he sat down by a well.

Fleeing from Egypt

On fleeing from Egypt Moses headed towards Midian. The route Moses took to Midian would have taken him through the Sinai wilderness.

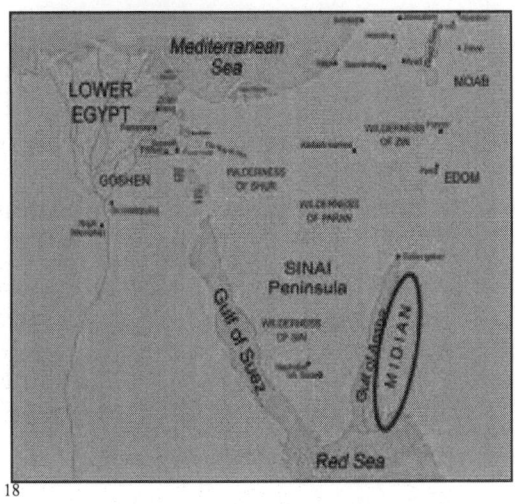

Moses' Flight and Return to Egypt

After killing the Egyptian, Moses fled through Sinai and settled in Midian, where he married Zipporah. God spoke to Moses to Moses at the burning bush at Horeb, after which Moses returned to Egypt to assist the Israelites.

It is not known how long it took Moses to cross the Sinai Wilderness however, seeing he fled Egypt unprepared for the journey, we can assume he had nothing with him. Moses had not planned to flee Egypt that day, so he would not have had the necessary sustaining items to keep him on his long journey. A wilderness is a place where one can find deadly creatures, such as snakes, scorpions,

---

[18] Esword Bible Study Commentary—Gill

desert foxes and lizards. On a terrain where there is no water and hardly any food, it is a life or death situation, and to survive one cannot sit idly. The heat of the sun can prove to be as deadly as the sting of a snake or scorpion. Going through the wilderness will also drain the body of fluids; for not having any water to quench his parched lips; Moses would be dehydrated and if he was walking, as it would have taken many days to cross such a hostile terrain. Moses was travelling alone, another situation where he would have to find the strength to push through against the odds, regardless of how tired, dehydrated, drained, weak, hot, cold, hungry or thirsty he was. He could not afford to stop for long periods as he was prone to all manner of attacks, being by himself. Being beaten upon by the elements, without any food or water, he must have been very weak by the time he made it to Midian. Moses encountered two wilderness experiences in his life and would soon embark upon a third:

1. His flight from Egypt to Midian
2. His downfall from his place of prominence in Egypt
3. His leading of the children of Israel through the wilderness

Moses had survived his first wilderness experience, making it from Egypt to Midian. Though weak, weary, parched from thirst and even hungry, he had gone through the wilderness and arrived in Midian. What he left Egypt with, had sustained him for the duration (which is not mentioned) of his journey.

Moses also survived the second wilderness experience, which was not physical but more a positional one. He was referred to as "Prince of Egypt", he was being groomed to rule, he was in a place of prominence, having power with those who ruled Egypt. But that all changed, he was struck from their list of would be successors, the very tomb which was being built for him was halted. As was the custom, the prince of Egypt would have their tombs built in advance of their death, it is recorded that when Moses fled Egypt, work stopped on his tomb. The statues, which were being built to reflect his prominence and position ceased, some were even defaced and destroyed. No further mention was made of Moses in the Egyptian writings or hieroglyphics; it was as if he had fallen off the face of the earth. The once "Prince of Egypt, had become an outcast, with a death warrant on his head. If he were to ever return while the Pharaoh who had decreed his death was alive, his punishment would be certain death. The third wilderness experience for Moses will be looked at in more detail in the following chapter.

Questions for Chapter 5:

1. Apart from Moses, name three (3) others who experienced a positional wilderness experience.

2. Investigate the circumstances surrounding one (1) of those you have named and give details as to the

   a. Situation leading up to the positional wilderness experience

   b. Cause for such an experience

   c. Result or outcome after the experience

   Please provide Bible scripture and references for your answers.

3. Have you ever suffered a positional wilderness Experience? If so, then:

   a. Give details of the experience

   b. Share your personal testimony as to:

      i. What you learned from the experience

      ii. What aided you while going through the experience

      iii. Would you be able to encourage someone else going through a positional wilderness? If so, say how? If not, say why not?

Exodus 10:2

*And that thou mayest tell it in the ears of thy son, and of
thy son's son, what things I have wrought in Egypt, and my
signs which I have done among them; that they may know
how that I am the LORD*

CHAPTER 6

*"Wilderness Experience
The Children of Israel"*

From the offspring of Jacob; Reuben, Simeon, Levi, Judah,
Issachar, Zebulun, Benjamin, Dan, Naphtali, Gad and Asher, those
who had moved to Egypt (Joseph was already in Egypt), because
of the famine that was in the land. Staying in Egypt some almost
one hundred and forty-six years and many generations later, they
had been placed in bondage. Over four hundred years later, God
would send a deliverer to their aid. The deliverer had been trained
in the courts of the Pharaoh's.

[19]This deliverer would be none other than Moses. Moses
would have been taught at least three different languages,
Egyptian, Akkadian and Hebrew, making him proficient in
communication.

He had an encounter with the God of heaven, while watching a
burning bush which the fire did not consume, this led Moses to

---

[19] The Nelson's Study Bible - NKJV

the one True and Living God. This was an important meeting, as Moses being accustomed to the Egyptians worship of many gods (polytheistic) and each god in Egypt had a name, which was associated with something in nature. Each Egyptian god also had an associated symbol, appearance and nature (as depicted by the chart below). It was imperative therefore, for God to bring Moses to the realisation that there is only one True God. Moses being accustomed to each god being associated with a symbol in nature and a name, Moses wanted to know the name of this "Hebrew God", hence he asked God's name. He was taught about the God of Abraham, the God of Isaac, the God of Jacob, hence his curiosity, fuelled by his custom, led to the question about God's name.

Exo 3:13   And Moses said unto God, Behold, when I come unto the children of Israel, and shall say unto them, The God of your fathers hath sent me unto you; and they shall say to me, What is his name? what shall I say unto them?

Exo 3:14   And God said unto Moses, I AM THAT I AM: and he said, Thus shalt thou say unto the children of Israel, I AM hath sent me unto you.

[20]Egyptian Idols

God of	Name	Appearance	Symbol	Nature
Sun	Ra	head of falcon and sun disk	White Crown	Cobra
Music	Hathor	horns of cow and sun disk	Red Crown	Falcon
Destruction	Sekhmet	head of lion	Eye Horus	Ibis
Sky	Nut	blue with golden stars	Feather of Ma'at	Scarab beetle
Earth	Geb	colour of plants and Nile mud	Ankh	Moon
Dead	Osiris	dressed in white with crook and flail	Sceptre of Seth	Ram
Desert	Seth	animal head with long curved snout	Sun Disk	Ammonite
Pharaoh	Horus	head of hawk and crown of Egypt	Boat of Ra	
Magic	Isis	throne on head or holding baby	Crook and Flail	
Wisdom	Thoth	head of ibis	Scarab	
Embalming	Anubis	head of jackal		
Justice	Ma'at	feather in her hair	Monsters	
Creation	Amun	crowned with feathers	Ammit the destroyer	
Cats	Baster	head of cat	Apep the snake	

This experience introduced Moses to a moving, living God, not one that was sat on a statue or was carved out by man's hand. But rather the God that could not be seen, could not be touched, yet who did wonders, like Moses had never seen in Egypt.

Armed with his new found belief and experience; Moses began his return to Egypt, this time as the called out and chosen deliverer of his brethren. Knowing that the impending threat of being killed which was looming over him, had now subsided [21]for it was the custom of Egypt, that when a Pharaoh died, all pending charges were dropped. Therefore, with the death of Tutmoses II, Moses could safely make his return to Egypt.

God looked upon the children of Israel, he heard their cry,

---

[20] Nelson's Study Bible - NKJV
[21] http://gwydir.demon.co.uk/jo/egypt/index.htm

acknowledged their pain and remembered them. Time had come for them to be delivered. The word he had spoken to Abraham (Gen 15:13-14) so many hundreds of years previous was about ready to be fulfilled.

Through various visits to Pharaoh and diverse miracles, the Bible records the children of Israel came out of Egypt with substance. (Gen 15:14) God delivered them with a strong arm.

The Start of the Deliverance

Pharaoh pronounced death upon Moses should he come back into his presence, and Moses, with full assurance agreed that Pharaoh would not see his face any more.

> Exo 10:28   And Pharaoh said unto him, Get thee from me, take heed to thyself, see my face no more; for in that day thou seest my face thou shalt die.
>
> Exo 10:29   And Moses said, Thou hast spoken well, I will see thy face again no more.

This boldness was due to the fact that God had given Moses the information that yet one more plague was to be brought upon Egypt, one that would affect all of Egypt, from Pharaoh's house to the lowest of the nation, even unto the beast of their field.

> Exo 11:5   And all the firstborn in the land of Egypt shall die, from the firstborn of Pharaoh that sitteth upon his throne, even unto the firstborn of the maidservant that is behind the mill; and all the firstborn of beasts.
>
> Exo 11:6   And there shall be a great cry throughout

all the land of Egypt, such as there was none
like it, nor shall be like it any more.

However, this would be a sign of great separation between
Egypt and Israel, for God had caused various plagues before
which had not affected Israel, however, this would show even
more so, the social opposites, that God had put on Egypt and
Israel, for while none of the Egyptians would escape the plague,
none of Israel would be affected.

Through the covering of the blood on the door posts, Israel sat
ready to be thrust out of Egypt, because God had given them the
word to be prepared to leave. They had borrowed all the gold they
needed, they had eaten the Passover dressed to leave. This is
significant of the church, being ready for the rapture in a sinful
world. For though we are in the world, we are not of the world,
the children of Israel were in Egypt, but it was evident from the
way they were treated by Egypt, the distinct separation of making
them slaves also and more importantly, the way the separation
was made by God; sending ten (10) plagues upon Egypt, none of
which affected the Israelites. Egypt thought themselves better
than the Hebrews, but God would show up and make the most
significant separation; for it is what God thinks that really matters.

The church too is in this world but not of the world, we
ought to be more concerned with what God thinks, for the Lord
does instruct us that in an hour when we think not, the Son of
man shall appear, therefore, we should be ready.

Mat 24:44   *Therefore be ye also ready: for in such an hour*
as ye think not the Son of man cometh.

God has set a distinct separation between the world and the church. We ought to remember that we are a royal priesthood, chosen generation, a peculiar people, a holy nation, one that should always be showing forth the praises of Him who hath called us out of darkness (the bondage of Egypt), into his marvelous light (1Peter 2:9).

Heading For the Wilderness

In that self-same night, God brought Israel out of Egypt. Their deliverance from slavery would take them on a trip through the wilderness for forty years, where most of them, all but two would die, not because that was what God had intended, but because they misunderstood what God was doing with them, they had not changed their mindset, embracing the transition. They had been in bondage for so long, they no longer could recognise a blessing, they had grown accustomed to being told what to do, having their meal time set, having their meal given to them. For they were slaves, and slaves would be told what time to eat, would have their meal controlled, they could only eat what was left from their task masters' table. They were told when to rise, were chastised if the job was not done well. Their minds had been trapped in a slave mentality, so though they had been delivered, their minds were still trapped.

It is vital for us as children of God to understand what God is doing. Even if we don't know the detail, know that his thoughts toward us are peace and not evil (Jeremiah 29:11). It is also vital to recognise where we are in our walk with God. For if we miss where we are, we could get frustrated with God, having the wrong expectations. If we are aware that we are going through a wilderness, then we would ensure certain things: whether the journey was planned or unplanned, we must

1. Check our resources or sustenance: for there may be bouts of long travel without any means of nourishment. Therefore, what we already have (when entering the wilderness), needs to be utilized in such a way, that allows it to last the course of the duration in the wilderness, and not run out too quickly, as we may be in the wilderness longer than anticipated.

2. Try to travel as fast as we can in the day light, as night time in the wilderness is dark and dangerous. The intention is to get out of the wilderness as quickly and as safely as possible. Also, it is difficult to travel over rough unchartered territory in the dark, as you could find yourself plunging to your death, because you walked off a cliff in the dark.

3. Ensure that you are protected from danger as best as possible. For the longer you are in the wilderness, the more tired and weak you will grow. Be aware of what is around you and like the Eagle, stay where you will not become prey to other wilderness creatures.

The Bible records that God did not lead the children of Israel through the land of the Philistines, although that route was nearer. God knew that if the Israelites saw war, they may run back to Egypt. God strategically planned their route, to ensure they would not desire to go back into bondage.

> Exo 13:17   *And it came to pass, when Pharaoh had let the*
> *people go, that God led them not through the way*
> *of the land of the Philistines, although that*
> *was near; for God said, Lest peradventure the*
> *people repent when they see war, and they*
> *return to Egypt:*

The Children of Israel started out on their journey, God was evidently with them. He manifested as a pillar of cloud by day, leading them and a pillar of fire by night, offering protection and warmth, they could see him visibly. The miracles God performed before the Israelites were so many and they did not stop in Egypt. God had proven himself to them so many times already in Egypt, on their journey out of Egypt and getting to the Red Sea. He separated the camp of Israel from the oncoming wrath of Pharaoh, allowing them all to safely walk through on dry land, parting the Red Sea. Their journey from there should have taken eleven days (11)

> Deu 1:2   (There are eleven days' journey from Horeb
> by the way of mount Seir unto
> Kadeshbarnea).

[22]The Israelites were eleven days in going from Horeb to Kadesh-barnea, where they were near the verge of the promised land; after which they were thirty-eight years wandering up and down in the vicinity of this place, not being permitted, because of their rebellion, to enter into the promised rest, though they were the whole of that time within a few miles of the land of Canaan!

---

[22] The Nelson's Study Bible Notes

The Children of Israelite's Mindset

Why then was Israel wondering around in the desert. They got to the Promised Land! They only needed to go forward and possess the promise God had set before them. God knowing that they had to travel through the wilderness would not have planned a journey of forty years for a wilderness. For in a wilderness, you have to be sustained with what you already have. There is no provision in the wilderness to add to you but rather, to take from you. Everything you bring with you into the wilderness must be sufficient to keep you, from the elements, the wild animals, the terrain, the arid land and the cold nights. It was God's will for them to exile Egypt and soon after enter the Promised Land.

A mindset of fear crippled their future possession. After all they had seen God do, they failed to retain God in their minds. After he had kept his word to deliver them and sent the deliverer, protected them whilst in Egypt from the Egyptians, protected them from Pharaoh and protected them from the plagues, after God had delivered them with a strong arm, ensuring they left Egypt with possessions more than they would ever dream, with enough gold to support them where they were going. After He visibly stayed by them, as a pillar of cloud by day to give them full assurance of his leading, a fire by night to provide them with light and protection in the night, after he had miraculously parted the Red Sea, causing them to walk through on dry land, allowing for enough time for approximately two to three million people to cross over whilst keeping back the armies of Pharaoh at the same time and holding back the waters of the sea.

> *Exo 14:20*   *And it came between the camp of the Egyptians and the camp of Israel; and it was a cloud and darkness to them, but it gave light by night to these: so that the one came not near the other all the night.*
>
> *Exo 14:21*   *And Moses stretched out his hand over the sea; and the LORD caused the sea to go back by a strong east wind all that night, and made the sea dry land, and the waters were divided.*
>
> *Exo 14:22*   *And the children of Israel went into the midst of the sea upon the dry ground: and the waters were a wall unto them on their right hand, and on their left.*

Not only that, but in the morning the Israelites could see the bodies of the Egyptians on the bank of the Red Sea. God had fought for them and had triumphed over their enemies, killing their oppressors.

> *Exo 14:23*   *And the Egyptians pursued, and went in after them to the midst of the sea, even all Pharaoh's horses, his chariots, and his horsemen.*
>
> *Exo 14:28*   *And the waters returned, and covered the chariots, and the horsemen, and all the host of Pharaoh that came into the sea after them; there remained not so much as one of them.*
>
> *Exo 14:29*   *But the children of Israel walked upon dry land in the midst of the sea; and the waters were a wall unto them on their right hand, and on their left.*
>
> *Exo 14:30*   *Thus the LORD saved Israel that day out of the hand of the Egyptians; and Israel saw the Egyptians dead upon the sea shore.*
>
> *Exo 14:31*   *And Israel saw that great work which the LORD did upon the Egyptians: and the people feared the LORD, and believed the LORD, and his servant Moses.*

Wilderness Warnings

When God is bringing you through a wilderness, it is a transition from one place to another. Moving you while stripping you down to your last to refill you, rejuvenate and revive you. It is not for you to desire the things from which he has taken you or to look back, regrettably, wanting to experience what you had left behind. We see this clearly in the story of Sodom and Gomorrah, the instruction Lot received for himself and his family was clear.

> *Gen 19:15*   *And when the morning arose, then the angels hastened Lot, saying, Arise, take thy wife, and thy two daughters, which are here; lest thou be consumed in the iniquity of the city.*
>
> *Gen 19:16*   *And while he lingered, the men laid hold upon his hand, and upon the hand of his wife, and upon the hand of his two daughters; the LORD being merciful unto him: and they brought him forth, and set him without the city.*
>
> *Gen 19:17*   *And it came to pass, when they had brought them forth abroad, that he said, Escape for thy life; look not behind thee, neither stay thou in all the plain; escape to the mountain, lest thou be consumed.*

Look not behind thee, lest thou be consumed. Look not behind refers to physically looking back, or having the desire in your heart to go back or become regretful about what has been left behind. When God delivers us from somewhere and transitions us to another place, physically or spiritually, it is for us to embrace what God has done and not desire to go back.

> *Heb 10:38*   *Now the just shall live by faith: but if any man*

draw back, my soul shall have no pleasure in him.

Hebrews 10:38 makes it clear to us that God does not take pleasure in those that draw back, those that desire the things from which you have been delivered. We should not desire the things of the world anymore, once we have been saved. Just as Israel should not have desired the things of Egypt anymore, for God had delivered them with a mighty arm. However, soon after, all those miracles, Israel lost heart and did the one thing that God did not want them to do, they desired to go back into bondage!

> *Exo 16:3*   *And the children of Israel said unto them, Would to God we had died by the hand of the LORD in the land of Egypt, when we sat by the flesh pots, and when we did eat bread to the full; for ye have brought us forth into this wilderness, to kill this whole assembly with hunger.*

The children of Israel murmured about everything, they murmured for lack of water,

> *Exo 15:22*   *So Moses brought Israel from the Red sea, and they went out into the wilderness of Shur; and they went three days in the wilderness, and found no water.*
>
> *Exo 15:23*   *And when they came to Marah, they could not drink of the waters of Marah, for they were bitter: therefore the name of it was called Marah.*
>
> *Exo 15:24*   *And the people murmured against Moses, saying, What shall we drink?*

They murmured for food,

Exo 16:3   *And the children of Israel said unto them, Would to God we had died by the hand of the LORD in the land of Egypt, when we sat by the flesh pots, and when we did eat bread to the full; for ye have brought us forth into this wilderness, to kill this whole assembly with hunger.*

They murmured for meat,

Num 11:4   *And the mixt multitude that was among them fell a lusting: and the children of Israel also wept again, and said, Who shall give us flesh to eat?*

Num 11:5   *We remember the fish, which we did eat in Egypt freely; the cucumbers, and the melons, and the leeks, and the onions, and the garlick:*

Num 11:6   *But now our soul is dried away: there is nothing at all, beside this manna, before our eyes.*

Num 11:31   *And there went forth a wind from the LORD, and brought quails from the sea, and let them fall by the camp, as it were a day's journey on this side, and as it were a day's journey on the other side, round about the camp, and as it were two cubits high upon the face of the earth.*

Num 11:32   *And the people stood up all that day, and all that night, and all the next day, and they gathered the quails: he that gathered least gathered ten homers: and they spread them all abroad for themselves round about the camp.*

Num 11:33   *And while the flesh was yet between their teeth, ere it was chewed, the wrath of the LORD was kindled against the people, and the LORD smote the people with a very great plague.*

They murmured for thirst,

Exo 17:3   *And the people thirsted there for water; and the people murmured against Moses, and said, Wherefore is this that thou hast brought us up out of Egypt, to kill us and our children and our cattle with thirst?*

And when they got to the Promised Land, they murmured about entering in. That proved to be one murmur too many.

> Num 13:25   *And they returned from searching of the land after forty days.*
>
> Num 13:26   *And they went and came to Moses, and to Aaron, and to all the congregation of the children of Israel, unto the wilderness of Paran, to Kadesh; and brought back word unto them, and unto all the congregation, and shewed them the fruit of the land.*
>
> Num 13:27   *And they told him, and said, We came unto the land whither thou sentest us, and surely it floweth with milk and honey; and this is the fruit of it.*
>
> Num 13:28   *Nevertheless the people be strong that dwell in the land, and the cities are walled, and very great: and moreover we saw the children of Anak there.*
>
> Num 13:29   *The Amalekites dwell in the land of the south: and the Hittites, and the Jebusites, and the Amorites, dwell in the mountains: and the Canaanites dwell by the sea, and by the coast of Jordan.*
>
> Num 13:30   *And Caleb stilled the people before Moses, and said, Let us go up at once, and possess it; for we are well able to overcome it.*
>
> Num 13:31   *But the men that went up with him said, We be not able to go up against the people; for they are stronger than we.*
>
> Num 13:32   *And they brought up an evil report of the land which they had searched unto the children of Israel, saying, The land, through which we have gone to search it, is a land that eateth up the inhabitants thereof; and all the people that we saw in it are men of a great stature.*
>
> Num 13:33   *And there we saw the giants, the sons of Anak, which come of the giants: and we were in our own sight as*
> *grasshoppers, and so we were in their sight.*

The children of Israel had gotten to the brink of Canaan, the land of Promise. God had brought them through the wilderness and to the edge, all they needed to do now was complete the journey by entering in and possess it, as God had promised them. Had God proven himself to them? Yes he had. Had he broken any of his word? No he had not. So what was it that caused Israel to get so far, yet perish in the wilderness?

They took it upon themselves to check out the land before occupying. I believe that if they had not sent the spies in before, but had all gone into the land, as God had instructed them, the story would have been very different. But they decided to send in the spies to spy out the land and bring back report. God had already told them that the land flowed with milk and honey. God had told them and shown them that he was with them, yet for reasons, I can only speculate, they sent in the ten spies. Ten of the twelve reported evil whilst only two reported good news. The people being accustomed to being under bondage by another nation lost heart forgot that God had promised the land to them and decided to murmur about the blessing that God had so richly provided, they refused to enter the land. They refused to grab a hold of the promise.

Num 14:1   *And all the congregation lifted up their voice, and cried; and the people wept that night.*
Num 14:2   *And all the children of Israel murmured against Moses and against Aaron: and the whole congregation said unto them, Would God that we had died in the land of Egypt! or would God we had died in this wilderness!*
Num 14:3   *And wherefore hath the LORD brought us unto*

this land, to fall by the sword, that our wives and our children should be a prey? were it not better for us to return into Egypt?

Num 14:4   *And they said one to another, Let us make a captain, and let us return into Egypt.*

Num 14:5   *Then Moses and Aaron fell on their faces before all the assembly of the congregation of the children of Israel.*

Num 14:6   *And Joshua the son of Nun, and Caleb the son of Jephunneh, which were of them that searched the land, rent their clothes:*

Num 14:7   *And they spake unto all the company of the children of Israel, saying, The land, which we passed through to search it, is an exceeding good land.*

Num 14:8   *If the LORD delight in us, then he will bring us into this land, and give it us; a land which floweth with milk and honey.*

Num 14:9   *Only rebel not ye against the LORD, neither fear ye the people of the land; for they are bread for us: their defence is departed from them, and the LORD is with us: fear them not.*

Num 14:10   *But all the congregation bade stone them with stones.*

And the glory of the LORD appeared in the tabernacle of the congregation before all the children of Israel.

Num 14:11   *And the LORD said unto Moses, How long will this people provoke me? and how long will it be ere they believe me, for all the signs which I have shewed among them*

How can we compare the promises of God to the things of the world? How can we who have been enlightened, have tasted of the heavenly gift, been made to partake of the Holy Ghost the word of God and the powers of the world to come, then turn around and choose the things of the world above the things of God? For often times, that is what we ourselves do. But thank God for his great mercy and his grace that covers us, so that we are not consumed.

The Children of Israel chose the things from which God had taken them, and they all died in the wilderness, for God's wrath was greatly kindled against them, and his patience ran short with them. He swore in wrath that they would not see nor enter the Promised Land. Over two million people died in the wilderness because they allowed fear to dictate their next move, which caused them to make the wrong decision, forfeiting the promise that was theirs to possess.

Num 14:20   *And the LORD said, I have pardoned according to thy word:*

Num 14:21   *But as truly as I live, all the earth shall be filled with the glory of the LORD.*

Num 14:22   *Because all those men which have seen my glory, and my miracles, which I did in Egypt and in the wilderness, and have tempted me now these ten times, and have not hearkened to my voice;*

Num 14:23   *Surely they shall not see the land which I sware unto their fathers, neither shall any of them that provoked me see it:*

Num 14:24   *But my servant Caleb, because he had another spirit with him, and hath followed me fully, him will I bring into the land whereinto he went; and his seed shall possess it.*

God swore in his wrath and once the word of God goes forth, it cannot return unto him void, but it must accomplish the thing to which it has been sent.

Isa 55:10   *For as the rain cometh down, and the snow from heaven, and returneth not thither, but watereth the earth, and maketh it bring forth and bud, that it may give seed to the sower, and bread to the eater:*

Isa 55:11   *So shall my word be that goeth forth out of my mouth: it shall not return unto me void, but it shall accomplish that which I please, and it shall prosper in the thing whereto I sent it.*

The word had gone forth, their punishment was set, and nothing could change it.

This is particularly sad, for how many times do we get to a place where we are at the brink of our promise, one step away from exiting our wildernesses, and we lose hope, and turn back to the things from which we had been called and delivered.

I pray, from this day forth, that we will not lose hope in our wildernesses, but endure, for God has no pleasure in them that draw back, and He is faithful and righteous, not giving us anything that we cannot be victorious

in.

Moses, who had survived his first wilderness, (running from Egypt) and his second (journeying back to Egypt as the deliverer) wilderness experience, also died in the wilderness. Moses was not allowed to enter the Promised Land, though he was allowed to see it. His third wilderness experience (leading the children of Israel from Egypt) would be his last, for though he was God's prophet and servant, the chosen deliverer for Israel, he, like all the others did not enter the Promise; whilst for differing reasons, Israel because of their unbelief and Moses, because he spoke in his wrath to God's people. Over two million people left Egypt, but only two entered into the Promised Land, Joshua and Caleb. The two who were among the the twelve spies who were confident that they, the Israelites could go into the promise that God had given them.

> *Num 13:30   And Caleb stilled the people before Moses, and said, Let us go up at once, and possess it; for we are well able to overcome it.*

Moses, the deliverer sent by God to lead the children of Israel out of Egypt, died in Moab at one hundred and twenty years old, having seen but not entering the Promised Land.

Moses 80		Moses 120
1445 B.C.		1405 B.C.
1 Ki 6:1	Num 32:13	Deu 34:7
Leads Exodus from Egypt	40 Years spent in the wilderness	Dies in Moab
Tutmoses IV (not first born)	Akhenaten (changes religion)	

Questions for Chapter 6:

God had chosen Moses as the deliverer of Israel. The plan and original intent of God was that Moses and the children of Israel would inherit the land of Canaan. However, from the scriptures we know that Moses and all of Israel, save Joshua and Caleb died in the wilderness, not inheriting the Promised Land.

Considering this:

1. What are some of the things that could hinder us obtaining what has been promised us?
2. How can we ensure that we obtain what God has promised us?
3. In your personal walk with God, did you ever get to the brink of what God has in store for you, but did not inherit it due to a bad decision? If yes, please give details. If no, then elaborate on how you have been successful in obtaining your promise.

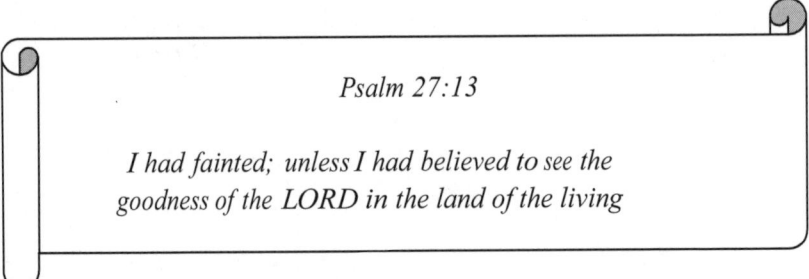

Psalm 27:13

*I had fainted; unless I had believed to see the
goodness of the LORD in the land of the living*

CHAPTER 7

"Wilderness Experience—David"

David, burst on to the scene as a young boy, in chapter 16 of 1 Samuel, and it was quite evident that he loved God. He was always writing God love poems, as evidenced by the seventy-two psalms he wrote to God. He was also a skillful harpist who would send up heart moving worship music to God. A keeper of his father's sheep, it signified that God was grooming him for something great in his future, David just didn't know it at the time. Anointed by Samuel the Prophet, secretly with only his family knowing, God hand selected David from his brethren. With the Spirit of God departing from the king at that time, being Saul, as a result of God's rejection of him, the Bible records that the Spirit of the Lord came upon David from that day on.

> *1Sa 16:13*   *Then Samuel took the horn of oil, and anointed him in the midst of his brethren: and the Spirit of the LORD came upon David from that day forward. So Samuel rose up, and went to Ramah.*

> *1Sa 16:14   But the Spirit of the LORD departed from Saul,*
> *and an evil spirit from the LORD troubled him.*

David's musical genius brought him into the palace to play for the king. King Saul was being troubled by an evil spirit, and sometimes seemed to suffer from bouts of insanity. Advised by some of his men, that what he needed was someone to play for him, so that his melancholy could be soothed, he accepted and instructed them to find him a player.

> *1Sa 16:16   Let our lord now command thy servants, which are*
> *before thee, to seek out a man, who is a cunning*
> *player on an harp: and it shall come to pass,*
> *when the evil spirit from God is upon thee, that*
> *he shall play with his hand, and thou shalt be*
> *well.*
> *1Sa 16:17   And Saul said unto his servants, Provide me now*
> *a man that can play well, and bring him to me.*

One of them reported that they had witnessed David's playing and thought he would be suitable, because the Lord was with him.

> *1Sa 16:18   Then answered one of the servants, and*
> *said, Behold, I have seen a son of Jesse the*
> *Bethlehemite, that is cunning in playing, and a*
> *mighty valiant man, and a man of war, and*
> *prudent in matters, and a comely person, and the*
> *LORD is with him.*
> *1Sa 16:19   Wherefore Saul sent messengers unto Jesse, and*
> *said, Send me David thy son, which is with the*
> *sheep.*

Saul gave word to send for him and so David soon started playing for Saul. David's playing brought peace to Saul therefore, he was often in the palace. God's rejection of Saul did not mean an immediate end of Saul's reign. He was still the king and David was still a shepherd boy, but one who knew, he was anointed to be king. He had no specific details as to when his ruling would begin, but he knew he was anointed to be king.

David Encounters Goliath

David's skill and fearless war strategy became known in the battle between himself and the giant Goliath. In a stand-off between Israel and Philistine, which Goliath challenged Israel to settle by individual combat between their chosen best fighters. No one moved forward or volunteered from the army of Israel, because they would be up against a nine feet, nine (9) inches (with a cubit being 18 inches and a span [1]9 inches) giant. It is to be noted that the obvious choice to stand up and fight for Israel would have been king Saul, as when he was anointed king over Israel, the scripture records that he stood head and shoulders over his countrymen.

> 1Sa 9:2   *And he had a son, whose name was Saul, a choice young man, and a goodly: and there was not among the children of Israel a goodlier person than he: from his shoulders and upward he was higher than any of the people*

This meant therefore that Saul was quite tall, though maybe not as tall as Goliath. Goliath, the giant of a man was a decorated war hero of Philistine. He had a helmet of brass upon his head. [23]This would have been a helmet

---

[23] Esword Bible Study—Commentary Clarke

made of bronze, most other fighters had a leather helmet. Goliath was armed with a coat of mail weighing five thousand shekels in brass. [24]This coat of mail was made of overlapping plates of bronze sewn on leather. [25]This armour weighed close to or approximately one hundred and twenty-five pounds (one shekel is approximately 0.0251327lb). Goliath had greaves of brass upon his legs, a target of brass between his legs, which was bronze protection for his legs. Carrying a spear (much like a javelin designed for hand to hand combat) compared to that of a weaver's beam;

> [26]A weaver's beam: *(Either like that on which the warp is rolled, or that on which the cloth is rolled. We know not how thick this was, because there were several sorts of looms, and the sizes of the beams very dissimilar. Our woollen, linen, cotton, and silk looms are all different in the size of their beams; and supposedly too thick, though they might be too short, for Goliath's spear.)*

of which the head of the spear weighed six hundred shekels of iron (or about 17lbs) and one went before him carrying his shield, meaning Goliath had his own shield bearer. Now that sight must have been quite intimidating.

One man, Goliath, because of his stature and war outfit, had taunted and drove fear into the entire army of Israel. No one was willing to fight him, but David rose to the challenge. Still only a lad, king Saul in his insanity, allowed a boy to represent Israel. Everyone else thought this would

---

[24] The Nelson Study Bible Notes
[25]The Nelson Study Bible Notes
[26]E-Sword commentary—Clarke

mean the sure death of David, for not only was he yet a boy, he had no formal training in war or individual combat. If the trained soldiers couldn't stand up to Goliath with all their armour and fittings, how could David with no protective armour or clothing and armed with only a child's toy. Goliath thought it an insult and a mockery, Israel thought it insanity and sure death for David, but David thought it an opportunity to prove to all Israel and the Philistines that the God of Israel was to be feared and no one could defile the armies of the LORD. Armed with only a sling and some stones, David charged Goliath and threw a stone which God directed straight to the forehead of Goliath, bringing him down; where David used Goliath's own sword to decapitate him by removing his head and bringing it as a war trophy back to Jerusalem. This started the beginning of the end of Saul's admiration, appreciation and love for David.

The report of what David had done had spread like wild fire, the people of Israel began to cheer and celebrate David and in that celebration, they attributed thousands to Saul and tens of thousands to David, Saul was not pleased and from then on, decided that David should be killed as his living meant Jonathan, Saul's son would not rule the kingdom, but rather David. Because David had become the object of adulation by the women in Israel and the favourite in all Israel, even for the soldiers of Saul and the men of Israel, Saul's plot to kill David did not begin as an open plan but rather a secret one. For Saul had no justifiable reason to slay David, only that his enraged jealousy was driving him and so he would try to kill David as he played for him at first. His many attempts failed and this angered Saul the more and even more so as it seems Jonathan his own son and Michal his daughter choose to side with

David instead of leading him to a certain death at Saul their father's hand. Realising that Saul's intent to kill him was growing ever more determined, David started to hide and eventually ran from Saul. Saul would chase David for years.

David Goes to the Philistines

Over chapters 18 through to 26 of 1 Samuel, the chase of David by Saul can be followed, from Nob to Gath, the home of Goliath whom David had killed, to the caves of Adullam to Moab. From Moab to Hereath, from Hereath to Keilah, from Keilah to Ziph from Ziph to the Maon desert, south of Hebron. From Hebron to En Gedi, where David had the opportunity to kill his pursuer, but chose rather to leave the slaying of Saul to God. From En Gedi to the Judean deserts and back to Maon, from Maon back to Ziph, from Ziph to the Negev desert where once again, David could have ended this chase by doing away with his nemesis, but once again, David only showed Saul that he meant him no harm, though he had occasion to kill him, he would not lift his hand against him.

> *1Sa 26:9*   *And David said to Abishai, Destroy him not: for who can stretch forth his hand against the LORD'S anointed, and be guiltless?*
>
> *1Sa 26:10*   *David said furthermore, As the LORD liveth, the LORD shall smite him; or his day shall come to die; or he shall descend into battle, and perish.*
>
> *1Sa 26:11*   *The LORD forbid that I should stretch forth mine hand against the LORD'S anointed: but, I pray thee, take thou now the spear that is at his bolster, and the cruse of water, and let us go.*

Soon after David would set up camp at Ziklag, in the land of the

Philistines. The very enemies of David was who God would chose to use to provide a safe haven for David, as in the land of the Philistines, Saul could not chase him.

> *1Sa 27:1*   *And David said in his heart, I shall now perish one day by the hand of Saul: there is nothing better for me than that I should speedily escape into the land of the Philistines; and Saul shall despair of me, to seek me any more in any coast of Israel: so shall I escape out of his hand.*
>
> *1Sa 27:2*   *And David arose, and he passed over with the six hundred men that were with him unto Achish, the son of Maoch, king of Gath.*
>
> *1Sa 27:3*   *And David dwelt with Achish at Gath, he and his men, every man with his household, even David with his two wives, Ahinoam the Jezreelitess, and Abigail the Carmelitess, Nabal's wife.*
>
> *1Sa 27:4*   *And it was told Saul that David was fled to Gath: and he sought no more again for him.*

Being the place where Goliath whom he had slew hailed from, many would have remembered his act of slaying their war hero and might have wanted him dead. So in a bid to secure, not just his life but the life of the six hundred men and their families who had joined his flight; David made a deceptive deal with Achish, that he would join forces with them to fight against their common enemy, Israel. The same Israel that David had been anointed to rule over, albeit deceptive; as David and his men would carry out raids against the perennial enemies of Judah, while reporting to Achish on his return that he had raided Israel.

> *1Sa 27:5*   *And David said unto Achish, If I have now found grace in thine eyes, let them give me a place in*

> *some town in the country, that I may dwell there:*
> *for why should thy servant dwell in the royal city*
> *with thee?*
> 1Sa 27:6 *Then Achish gave him Ziklag that day: wherefore*
> *Ziklag pertaineth unto the kings of Judah unto this*
> *day.*

David experienced two (2) wilderness experiences prior to becoming king of Israel;

1. David experienced the Physical Wilderness and
2. The Positional Wilderness.

The Physical Wilderness

David had gone through the wildernesses of Moab, Judea, Ziph, Maon and En Gedi running from Saul, a seemingly never ending chase which took him across the whole region, from Moab to Engedi and back. He was forced to stay ahead of Saul, in position and in tactics, or it would have meant his life. Many times to ensure food and sustenance for he and his men, David would offer protection to those with livestock and goods from which he and his men could benefit, as the deserted areas yielded nothing with which they could sustain themselves.

The Positional Wilderness

Like Moses, David also experienced the wilderness of losing his influence. He was hailed in Israel as a warrior, one of the chief captains and best fighter. He was admired and loved by the people and desired by the women. He had gained the respect of the soldiers for not only did he slay Goliath, but he had killed one hundred Philistines by himself in a bid to marry the king's daughter, offering them as a dowry to the king, albeit a plot devised to bring about his demise. He had influence, power and authority. Now he was being chased as a commoner, treated as a common thief, regarded as a betrayer of the king, the king whom he had spent countless days with, soothing his ailment by playing skillfully upon a harp for, the king whom David had approached as a child, laying his life on the line to fight for Israel, and bringing victory to the king and all the land of Israel. Even the very people whom he had gone out on many occasions to fight for in protecting their borders were all too willing to pass information on to king Saul as to his whereabouts. On some occasion the Spirit of the Lord would forewarn him to leave where he was, as the people of that city would give him up to Saul. Many times as soon as he arrived there, they had sent words to Saul to come capture him. David had lost his place and position of power and his wilderness experience reduced him to live among his enemies, the Philistines.

1Sa 27:4	*And it was told Saul that David was fled to Gath: and he sought no more again for him.*
1Sa 27:5	*And David said unto Achish, If I have now found grace in thine eyes, let them give me a place in some town in the country, that I may dwell there: for why should thy servant dwell in the royal city with thee?*
1Sa 27:6	*Then Achish gave him Ziklag that day: wherefore Ziklag pertaineth unto the kings of Judah unto this day.*
1Sa 27:7	*And the time that David dwelt in the country of the Philistines was a full year and four months.*

God Saves David from Himself

This same David who had been anointed king, who had the privilege of knowing his future at a young age, that he would soon be crowned king of Israel, had made a declaration to Achish, arch enemy of Israel, that he, David, would slay as many Israelites as he could in battle, fighting side by side with Achish and the Philistines.

> *1Sa 28:1*   *And it came to pass in those days, that the Philistines gathered their armies together for warfare, to fight with Israel. And Achish said unto David, Know thou assuredly, that thou shalt go out with me to battle, thou and thy men.*
>
> *1Sa 28:2*   *And David said to Achish, Surely thou shalt know what thy servant can do. And Achish said to David, Therefore will I make thee keeper of mine head for ever.*
>
> *1Sa 29:1*   *Now the Philistines gathered together all their armies to Aphek: and the Israelites pitched by a fountain which is in Jezreel.*
>
> *1Sa 29:2*   *And the lords of the Philistines passed on by hundreds, and by thousands: but David and his men passed on in the rereward with Achish.*

The very nation David was anointed to rule over, protect and lead, he was now ready to kill. So great was his wilderness experience, for years; running from Saul and hiding in caves, being treated like a common thief and even having some of his countrymen turn against him, along with the wilderness of falling from a place of influence, that he was ready to go against the future that God had promised and given him a glimpse of.

However, God in his wisdom had a plan to save David from doing something that would cause Him (God) to turn around and destroy David. For God had declared his ownership of Israel and intent on fighting for them against any enemy or foe. David who had been chosen to rule Israel would have been destroyed by God, had he gone through with his decision to fight with the Philistines against Israel. God allowed the Princes of the Philistines to instruct Achish, whom David and his men were marching with to gather against Israel, to send David back to Ziklag, as they thought David could turn against them and betray them in the heat of the battle. David and his men had to therefore return to Ziklag.

> *1Sa 29:1* *Now the Philistines gathered together all their armies to Aphek: and the Israelites pitched by a fountain which is in Jezreel.*
>
> *1Sa 29:2* *And the lords of the Philistines passed on by hundreds, and by thousands: but David and his men passed on in the rereward with Achish.*
>
> *1Sa 29:3* *Then said the princes of the Philistines, What do these Hebrews here? And Achish said unto the princes of the Philistines, Is not this David, the servant of Saul the king of Israel, which hath been with me these days, or these years, and I have found no fault in him since he fell unto me unto this day?*
>
> *1Sa 29:4* *And the princes of the Philistines were wroth with him; and the princes of the Philistines said unto him, Make this fellow return, that he may go again to his place which thou hast appointed him, and let*

him not go down with us to battle, lest in the battle he be an adversary to us: for wherewith should he reconcile himself unto his master? should it not be with the heads of these men?

1Sa 29:5   *Is not this David, of whom they sang one to another in dances, saying, Saul slew his thousands, and David his ten thousands?*

1Sa 29:6   *Then Achish called David, and said unto him, Surely, as the LORD liveth, thou hast been upright, and thy going out and thy coming in with me in the host is good in my sight: for I have not found evil in thee since the day of thy coming unto me unto this day: nevertheless the lords favour thee not.*

1Sa 29:7   *Wherefore now return, and go in peace, that thou displease not the lords of the Philistines.*

1Sa 29:8   *And David said unto Achish, But what have I done? and what hast thou found in thy servant so long as I have been with thee unto this day, that I may not go fight against the enemies of my lord the king?*

1Sa 29:9   *And Achish answered and said to David, I know that thou art good in my sight, as an angel of God: notwithstanding the princes of the Philistines have said, He shall not go up with us to the battle.*

1Sa 29:10   *Wherefore now rise up early in the morning with thy master's servants that are come with thee: and as soon as ye be up early in the morning, and have light, depart.*

1Sa 29:11   *So David and his men rose up early to depart in the morning, to return into the land of the Philistines. And the Philistines went up to Jezreel.*

Even after returning to Ziklag, David could have decided to rejoin the Philistines in battle against Israel, however, God allowed the Amalekites to invade Ziklag and they took away everything that David and his men had looted, along with their wives and children.

1Sa 30:1   *And it came to pass, when David and his men were come to Ziklag on the third day, that the Amalekites had invaded the south, and Ziklag, and smitten Ziklag, and burned it with fire;*

1Sa 30:2   *And had taken the women captives, that were therein: they slew not any, either great or small, but carried them away, and went on their way.*

1Sa 30:3   *So David and his men came to the city, and, behold, it was burned with fire; and their wives, and their sons, and their daughters, were taken captives.*

1Sa 30:4   *Then David and the people that were with him lifted up their voice and wept, until they had no more power to weep.*

1Sa 30:5   *And David's two wives were taken captives, Ahinoam the Jezreelitess, and Abigail the wife of Nabal the Carmelite.*

1Sa 30:6   *And David was greatly distressed; for the people spake of stoning him, because the soul of all the people was grieved, every man for his sons and for his daughters: but David encouraged himself in the LORD his God.*

1Sa 30:7   *And David said to Abiathar the priest, Ahimelech's son, I pray thee, bring me hither the ephod. And Abiathar brought thither the ephod to David.*

1Sa 30:8   *And David enquired at the LORD, saying, Shall I pursue after this troop? shall I overtake them? And he answered him, Pursue: for thou shalt surely overtake them, and without fail recover all.*

1Sa 30:9   *So David went, he and the six hundred men that were with him, and came to the brook Besor, where those that were left behind stayed.*

David now had to concentrate on recapturing his family and possessions and that also of his men. God ensured that David would not have second thoughts about visiting the battleground and having to fight for Achish against Israel. God ensured that David would not be at the battleground at all. He and his men would have to pursue the invaders to recover their belongings and families. God had set David up to not go against his original intent of him being king over Israel, regardless of his wilderness experiences.

It is reassuring to know that God will do whatever he has to do to us, and for us, to ensure that we do not negate or abort his good intentions for us. God is committed to being the keeper of his words. For locked in the word of God is the innate compulsion to be accomplished. They are forbidden to return to him void. They must go forth and complete what they were sent to do. Truly, this is a reassuring relief, we can stand flat-footed upon the word of God for his words are in him yea and they are in him amen and he is the Promise Keeper.

Questions for Chapter 7:

1. Give another time in David's life when he experienced a positional wilderness experience
2. In no less than 500 words, give your explanation of the relevant scriptures and your understanding of the experience

Psalms 27:5

For in the time of trouble he shall hide me in his
pavilion: in the secret of his tabernacle shall he hide
me, he shall set me up upon a rock

CHAPTER 8

"Wilderness Experience—Job"

Job, whose name means "resting in the mystery of God" finds himself the protagonist between a Sovereign God and the tempter, Satan himself. Job is described as an upright, perfect man, who continually fears God and disdains evil. Job, blessed with a large family of seven sons and three daughters, and with livestock and wealth, did not lose sight of his godliness. This would move him to often make sacrifices, being vigilant regarding the spiritual wellbeing of his children.

God boasts on Job

Job 1:4   And his sons went and feasted *in their* houses, every one his day; and sent and called for their three sisters to eat and to drink with them.

Job 1:5   And it was so, when the days of *their* feasting were gone about, that Job sent and sanctified them, and rose up early in the morning, and offered burnt offerings *according* to the number of them all:

for Job said, It may be that my sons have sinned, and cursed God in their hearts. Thus did Job continually.

However, unknown to Job, God would hold him up before Satan as a model of righteousness on the earth. For though Satan had been given dominion over the fallen creation, and a temporary lordship over the earth, God used Job to remind Satan that his dominion was not complete and unexceptional, for here was Job, over who, Satan had no control.

Job 1:8   And the LORD said unto Satan, Hast thou considered my servant Job, that *there is* none like him in the earth, a perfect and an upright man, one that feareth God, and escheweth evil?

Satan's repartee was that Job was serving God basically for what he had received and Job had received much. Satan challenged God to remove the blessings and protection from Job's life and possessions, and watch Job curse him (God) to the face, as Job too would deny God's rule over him.

It is imperative for me at this juncture to point out that what the devil does is limited to what God allows. Whilst God has no evil in Him, he allows and uses evil or suffering, such as, illness, pain, death for his glory embracing it in his sovereignty. Though this may be difficult to understand from a theological stand point, to reject this is to accept the ideology of dualism. This is a belief in a "god of good" and a "god of evil", and that the two are locked in an irresolvable conflict. This belief is not only unfounded and not reflected in the word of God, but it also tries (if it were possible) to place an equality between God and Satan. This is erroneous, for that would be saying that the thing formed (Satan) had somehow risen to be greater than or equal to his creator (God). However, we know that with God or to God, there is no equal, none that can be likened or compared to Him. He is God all by himself and there is none else.

God granted Satan the permission to test his banter, giving him access to Job's possessions, children, goods and then later his flesh. In a series of cataclysmic disasters, happening in one day, Job lost everything. His oxen and asses were first to go along with the servants who were over them. Then the sheep and their servants, then the camels and their servants; and then his sons and daughters. In one day, with each event having just one servant left to report what had happened back to Job, everything that Job had; was gone **IN ONE DAY!**

Job 1:13	And there was a day when his sons and his daughters *were* eating and drinking wine in their eldest brother's house:
Job 1:14	And there came a messenger unto Job, and said, The oxen were plowing, and the asses feeding beside them:
Job 1:15	And the Sabeans fell *upon them,* and took them away; yea, they have slain the servants with the edge of the sword; and I only am escaped alone to tell thee.
Job 1:16	While he *was* yet speaking, there came also another, and said, The fire of God is fallen from heaven, and hath burned up the sheep, and the servants, and consumed them; and I only am escaped alone to tell thee.
Job 1:17	While he *was* yet speaking, there came also another, and said, The Chaldeans made out three bands, and

Job 1:18   fell upon the camels, and have carried them away, yea, and slain the servants with the edge of the sword; and I only am escaped alone to tell thee.

Job 1:18   While he *was* yet speaking, there came also another, and said, Thy sons and thy daughters *were* eating and drinking wine in their eldest brother's house:

Job 1:19   And, behold, there came a great wind from the wilderness, and smote the four corners of the house, and it fell upon the young men, and they are dead; and I only am escaped alone to tell thee.

Believer, Know Thyself

Now if that had not been enough, his friends were convinced he had sinned hence the judgment of God was being passed. Job's friends rebuked him for denying that he had sinned. They tried in every way to get Job to admit his wrong doings. They could not believe that the just God of heaven would have allowed the kind of disaster that was happening to occur without a reason. And they were right, just that the reason they thought was not the reason it happened. But that was not all, Job's wife, his companion and soul-mate, the person with whom he had shared his bed and his most intimate thoughts and secrets. The one person who should have known him and known enough to stand by his side, believing him when he said he had not sinned, knowing what God meant to him and understanding that his faith was all that he had left, this one person on whom Job depended for moral support and encouragement; she turned around and said the most shocking and foolish statement he had ever heard. She told Job to curse God and die. Did she not see the exemplary life Job lead? Yes she did, for she knew that if he were to curse God, he would die. I don't believe that she said this out of concern for Job, but more because she had become ashamed of him.

Job had seemingly fallen from a position of prominence. He was respected in the city gates. The men who sat in the city gates were judges, devout men, respected of the people. He was once very rich, now this man who once was overflowing with goods, livestock and wealth, had absolutely nothing. She enjoyed the prestige of being married to a wealthy man who was respected in the community. Now she also had to contend with the stares, even the ridicule of Job's new low status. Having seen her children, all ten of them, being buried maybe on the same day, whilst her husband held to a faith which she could not understand. Her pain proved greater than her hope in God. Having all their livestock, which in those days, represented wealth destroyed, and all those servants who perished along with the livestock, their families probably now wanted and sought for retribution. They wanted to blame someone she did not feel safe walking down the streets anymore. She no longer had the respect and envious stares of the other wives. She was now pointed at and could maybe sometimes even hear the whispers as she passed by. With her children dead, their livestock dead and gone, their wealth gone, their friends gone, in her frustration, and in a moment of weakness, she wished her husband also gone.

> Job 2:9   *Then said his wife unto him, Dost thou still retain thine integrity? curse God, and die.*
>
> Job 2:10   *But he said unto her, Thou speakest as one of the foolish women speaketh. What? shall we receive good at the hand of God, and shall we not receive evil? In all this did not Job sin with his lips.*

She could not believe that after everything that had happened, Job was still holding on to the God who would allow him to suffer in this way. She had obviously already blamed God.

Job had enough faith and courage to still find the strength to rebuke her for what she had thought and said. As he held firmly to his belief and his knowledge of God that what was happening to him was not because of sin, but for the will of God. This is often the hardest thing for us to think when we are going through a wilderness.

Job's Reward

When we are in a place of suffering, it takes great faith, it takes an unshaken belief in God, it takes a heart with absolutely no wavering or shadow of doubt. A full assurance of hope and faith in God, that he is not unrighteous, he is not tempted with evil, that God will not leave you comfortless, that when things go wrong, like they will sometimes do, that you have lived a life without sin, pleasing unto God, and that whatever happens to you, be it good or evil, that God allowed it for his glory.

This is a time when we must employ the scripture in 1 Thessalonians 5:18 which says:

> 1Th 5:18   In everything give thanks: for this is the will of God
> in Christ Jesus concerning you.

For yes, we know the story of Job and how it ended; God repaid Job, for all that he had endured. God gave him sons and daughters and much more livestock and wealth, greater than he had lost. However, this is where we often focused, on the end of Job, with all that he had, but before we can get to the end, where we are repaid with more than we lost, we must first go through the painful process of losing everything. Also, our mindset has to be so focused on giving God glory, that even if we do not reap a greater harvest at the end of it all, we still give him thanks for choosing us and thinking us worthy to be used by him to endure hardship and trials. Yes we know God is not unrighteous to forget our labour of love, however, we must love him and trust him so much that even if he chooses not to bless us, we will still be like Job, in saying, the Lord giveth and the Lord taketh away, blessed be the name of the Lord.

Questions for Chapter 8:

1. Apart from Job, can you name anyone else from the scriptures that lost everything and then regained it and more after enduring?

2. Compare and contrast five qualities that will aid you in regaining what you have lost and five qualities that will hinder you from regaining. Please provide scriptural references.

3. Can you give an example of a time when you lost everything and regained it?

4. Give details as to what you did and how you regained what you had lost?

Malachi 3:1

Behold, I will send my messenger, and he shall prepare the way before me: and the Lord, whom ye shall seek, shall suddenly come to his temple, even the messenger of the covenant, whom ye delight in: behold he shall come, saith the LORD of hosts.

CHAPTER 9

"Wilderness Experience—John the Baptist"

Introducing John the Baptist

Before I embark on this chapter about John the Baptist, I believe I must clear up which John I am writing about. First of all there are five men with the name John mentioned in the New Testament.

There is:

1. John the Baptist whose ministry spanned from around AD 25-27. He was known as "the voice", the forerunner of Jesus and was beheaded by Herod whilst in prison.
2. John the father of Peter (John 1:42)
3. John Mark (Acts 12:12), the author of the second gospel (St. Mark)
4. John of the Sanhedrin (Acts 4:5-6) an enemy of Christianity
5. John (the author of St. John) whose father was Zebedee and he was brother to James, a Galilean fishermen who was referred to in Matthew 4:21, as the disciple whom Jesus loved.

The John of whom I write, is the first John mentioned of the five, John the Baptist, who is not the author of St. John, though he is introduced in chapter one. St. John's references to John the Baptist in chapter 1:6-8, 15 & 19-28 can sometimes cause us to often confuse the two Johns. The references made of John the Baptist in the first chapter of St. John is pointing to the forerunner of Jesus Christ in the author's (St. John) introduction of the Messiah, Jesus Christ the anointed one.

Joh 1:6	*There was a man sent from God, whose name was John.*
Joh 1:7	*The same came for a witness, to bear witness of the Light, that all men through him might believe.*
Joh 1:8	*He was not that Light, but was sent to bear witness of that Light.*
Joh 1:15	*John bare witness of him, and cried, saying, This was he of whom I spake, He that cometh after me is preferred before me: for he was before me.*
Joh 1:19	*And this is the record of John, when the Jews sent priests and Levites from Jerusalem to ask him, Who art thou?*
Joh 1:20	*And he confessed, and denied not; but confessed, I am not the Christ.*
Joh 1:21	*And they asked him, What then? Art thou Elias? And he saith, I am not. Art thou that prophet? And he answered, No.*
Joh 1:22	*Then said they unto him, Who art thou? that we may give an answer to them that sent us. What sayest thou of thyself?*

Joh 1:23	*He said, I am the voice of one crying in the wilderness, Make straight the way of the Lord, as said the prophet Esaias.*
Joh 1:24	*And they which were sent were of the Pharisees.*
Joh 1:25	*And they asked him, and said unto him, Why baptizest thou then, if thou be not that Christ, nor Elias, neither that prophet?*
Joh 1:26	*John answered them, saying, I baptize with water: but there standeth one among you, whom ye know not;*
Joh 1:27	*He it is, who coming after me is preferred before me, whose shoe's latchet I am not worthy to unloose.*
Joh 1:28	*These things were done in Bethabara beyond Jordan, where John was baptizing.*

The author of St. John, number five in those mentioned before, his father is Zebedee. John the Baptist's father is Zachariah and his mother is Elisabeth, who is the cousin of Mary, the mother of Jesus, as detailed in St. Luke chapters one and three.

A Look at John's Descendants

It is recorded in the scriptures that both Zachariah and Elisabeth were righteous, walking in all the commandments and ordinances of the Lord, blameless. Both Zachariah and Elisabeth were of the tribe of Levi. Only those of the Levitical tribe were allowed to operate in the temple as priests and or high priests. For us to understand why of the twelve tribes of Israel, only one was chosen by God to serve him in the temple and priesthood, it is necessary for us to go back to the book of Exodus.

Choosing of the Levites

Chapter twenty-four of Exodus begins with God instructing Moses to bring with him Aaron, Nadab, Abihu and seventy of Israel's elders to commune with God in the Mountain. Moses, Aaron, Nadab, Abihu and the seventy elders took their journey up the mountain. Whilst in the mountain, God called for Moses to come up even higher to commune with him alone. Moses then journeyed even higher into the mountain taking Joshua, but only part of the way. Moses was by himself in the Mountain with God for forty days and nights.

The communion with God saw Moses being downloaded with all the instructions of the tabernacle and all its trappings, the altars, the different divisions (courtyard, inner court and most holy place) and all the differing items for each division. The ingredients and instruction for the anointing oil, the priest's garments, the curtains of the tabernacle and its varying colours, the length, width and height of each item of the courtyard columns. God gave specific details to Moses on everything regarding the temple and the priesthood, the offering altars, the shewbread, the candlestick, the incense oil and the mercy seat along with the offering necessary for sanctification of the priest prior to performing in that office. Every minute detail was given to Moses by God himself in this encounter; along with the original Ten Commandments. God even told Moses who had been anointed and endued with the knowledge and wisdom to make the items required in the tabernacle.

However, whilst Moses was receiving this instruction, being in the presence of God, it would seem that time ceased for Moses. Nine chapters later, some of the very things written in the ordinances of God were being broken. While God was giving the Laws to Moses, the children of Israel were at the same time breaking them. Let me pause to point out that Moses had brought Aaron, Nadab, Abihu, and seventy of their elders with him into the mountain. Moses and Joshua had carried on further, and then Joshua was left alone whilst Moses travelled on even further up the mountain. At some point, therefore, Aaron, Nadab, Abihu and the seventy elders must have returned down the mountain and had given up waiting on Moses. I believe that these seventy-three leaders were evidently unsettled about what had happened to Moses and this somehow translated to the people. For had the leaders been steadfast in believing that Moses was still yet alive and had exhibited confidence, standing as one voice to the people, they (the people) would have looked to the leaders for support and found strength in them to wait for Moses' return. But somehow I believe, they had shown and maybe even voiced their concern regarding Moses. The fact that they had left him in the mountain and with no word as to what had become of him, the people also became unsettled and lost confidence. Soon they approached Aaron, the high priest regarding their concerns and the high priest instructed them to break off their gold off their ears and with it Aaron, the high priest made a golden calf, as an idol for the people to worship, thereby committing idolatry. I point this out as evidence that no matter how close you are to someone (be it a leader, pastor, etc.), unless you have a relationship with God for yourself, you will revert to what you know in times of hardship.

Aaron, remember was the spokesperson for Moses set up by God, to speak to Pharaoh, as Moses had made excuses about his speech. Aaron was with Moses on various occasions when Moses approached Pharaoh. Aaron not only heard but was eyewitness to what God had done. He heard and sometimes participated in the conversations between Moses and Pharaoh. He also saw the signs and wonders, and when Moses spoke to God, that God would answer in no uncertain terms. Yet with all that Aaron witnessed, he never fully trusted God. For at a time when Moses was in the mountain and he was approached by the people, he could have redirected their attention back to God.

Aaron could have spoken up and declared as he had seen Moses do so many times, about this God who had brought them from such a mighty long way. Instead, Aaron, the High Priest, created an idol for the people to worship, causing Israel to commit an even greater sin of idolatry. Aaron though was not a leader, his mindset was still one of a slave, he had lived as a slave in Egypt for all those years before being freed from bondage. He had not yet been delivered from the enslaved mindset nor from the idolatrous worship that he had seen in Egypt. For the Egyptians who had ruled over them (Israel) worshipped idols. Their style of worship was polytheistic (having many gods/idols) and their idols were different statues sometimes having the body of a man and the head of different animals displayed in gold. [27]Gold was thought of in Egypt as being the flesh of the gods, a divine metal, therefore the statues of the Egyptian gods, goddesses, pharaohs and queens were made of gold. In making the golden calf, Aaron was reverting to his Egyptian knowledge and what he knew.

---

[27] *http://www.egyptiangods.co.uk/statues.htm*

God sent Moses down from the mountain as the people were committing idolatry, thereby corrupting themselves. Moses on arriving down the mountain, saw what Israel was doing, he became so angry that he threw down the tablets of stone upon which God had written the commandments, thereby breaking them. This was significant as man seemingly could not keep the law, man always more times than not, broke the law. Soon Moses had to stand between God and Israel to prevent God from destroying them. On that day, Moses asked a pivotal question there and then . . . "Who is on the LORD's side"? (Exodus 32:26)

> *Exo 32:26*   *Then Moses stood in the gate of the camp, and said, Who is on the LORD'S side? let him come unto me.*

Only the tribe of Levi moved forward. This was a very crucial question and the Levites' response gave them great importance with God. For prior to this, every firstborn of animal and man which opened the womb belonged to God, God had chosen them to be his. All unclean animals had to be redeemed, for they could not offer animals that were regarded as unclean as sacrifices to God and of course human sacrifice was not done. So these were redeemed using clean animals. This was what had been originally set up by God.

However, shortly after the incident with the golden calf, in Exodus chapter three, we see God make a switch, for now God had taken the Levites instead of all the firstborn. (Numbers 3:12-12)

> *Num 3:12*   *And I, behold, I have taken the Levites from among the children of Israel instead of all the firstborn that openeth the matrix among the children of*

> *Israel: therefore the Levites shall be mine;*
>
> *Num 3:13*   *Because all the firstborn are mine; for on the day that I smote all the firstborn in the land of Egypt I hallowed unto me all the firstborn in Israel, both man and beast: mine shall they be: I am the LORD.*

God made mention to the day he smote all the firstborn in Egypt, that he on that day hallowed all the firstborn in Israel, they were his, but now, he had taken the tribe of Levi, instead of the firstborn of all Israel. Hence the Levites were now hallowed unto the Lord. God instructed that only the Levites could do anything pertaining to the temple. Whether it was working on the inside of the temple, or transporting it from one place in the wilderness to another whilst on their journey, only the Levites were chosen to perform these tasks.

Zachariah's Course

Zachariah was of the course of Abia, which meant that he was of the eighth course of the Levites. In the time of David, when the family of Aaron was multiplied, he divided them into twenty-four courses, for the more regular performances of their office, that it might never be either *neglected* for want of hands or *engrossed* by a few. The eighth was *Abia* (*1Ch 24:10: the seventh was Hakkoz, the eighth was Abijah*), *(Abia or sometimes also known as Abijah)* who was descended from Eleazar, Aaron's eldest son. It is to be noted that, a priest would serve maybe for one week, twice a year, so this was a duty they waited for. Those serving started at age thirty according to 1 Chronicles 23:1-3

> *1Ch 23:1*   *So when David was old and full of days, he made Solomon his son king over Israel.*

> *1 Ch 23:2*   And he gathered together all the princes of Israel, with
> the priests and the Levites.
>
> *1 Ch 23:3*   Now the Levites were numbered from the age of thirty
> years and upward: and their number by their polls,
> man by man, was thirty and eight thousand.

Note also that the offering of the incense was something a priest could only ever do ***once*** in their life time. This was because of the vast number of Levites there were, and even though only Aaron's sons and those of their linage were able to serve in the temple, there were still thousands of them, and they all waited for their lot (time to serve). Moses' descendants, Gershon, Kohath and Merari, and their sons were chosen and divided to attend to other duties around the temple, but only Aaron and his sons could operate in the priesthood.

1 Chronicles 23 gives detail as to how many priests there were at the time that David numbered them. At that time the number of males above thirty years old in the Levitical tribe was thirty-eight thousand. Imagine so many waiting on their lot or time to serve in the temple. David divided them in such a way that the lot would fall on a particular section or lineage, at a particular time, giving them a better probability of one day serving in the temple. It is to be noted that not ALL the sons of Aaron were chosen to execute the priests' office. For as recorded in 1 Chronicles 24: 1-6, Aaron had four sons, they were Nadab, Abihu, Eleazar and Ithamar.

> *1 Ch 24:1*   Now these are the divisions of the sons of Aaron.
> The sons of Aaron; Nadab, and Abihu, Eleazar, and
> Ithamar.

Remember Nadab and Abihu died for offering strange fire before the Lord (Leviticus 10:1-2, Numbers 3:4 & Numbers 26:61)

Lev 10:1   *And Nadab and Abihu, the sons of Aaron, took either of them his censer, and put fire therein, and put incense thereon, and offered strange fire before the LORD, which he commanded them not.*

Lev 10:2   *And there went out fire from the LORD, and devoured them, and they died before the LORD.*

This left Eleazar and Ithamar's descendants to execute the office of the priesthood.

1Ch 24:2   *But Nadab and Abihu died before their father, and had no children: therefore Eleazar and Ithamar executed the priest's office.*

However, between them, the descendants of the Levites had grown to a vast number, (as mentioned before, thirty-eight thousand) when David numbered them. Therefore, David divided them. However, in the divisions, the sons of Eleazar were found to be more chief; meaning there were more leaders (chief men) found among the sons of Eleazar than of Ithamar. David took sixteen household of the sons of Eleazar and only eight from the sons of Ithamar to execute the priests' office.

1Ch 24:3   *And David distributed them, both Zadok of the sons of Eleazar, and Ahimelech of the sons of Ithamar, according to their offices in their service.*

1Ch 24:4   *And there were more chief men found of the sons of Eleazar than of the sons of Ithamar; and thus were they divided. Among the sons of Eleazar there were sixteen chief men of the house of their fathers, and eight among the sons of Ithamar according to the house of their fathers.*

1Ch 24:5   *Thus were they divided by lot, one sort with another;*

> for the governors of the sanctuary, and governors
> of the house of God, were of the sons of Eleazar,
> and of the sons of Ithamar.

1 Ch 24:6   And Shemaiah the son of Nethaneel the scribe, one
> of the Levites, wrote them before the king, and the
> princes, and Zadok the priest, and Ahimelech the son
> of Abiathar, and before the chief of the fathers of
> the priests and Levites: one principal household
> being taken for Eleazar, and one taken for
> Ithamar.

David divided them into twenty-four courses, 1 Chronicles 24: 1-19, namely:

Priestly 24 Course Division

1st	Jehoiarib	9th	Jeshua	17th	Hezir
2nd	Jedaiah	10th	Shecaniah	18th	Aphses
3rd	Harim	11th	Eliashib	19th	Pethahiah
4th	Seorim	12th	Jakim	20th	Jehezekel
5th	Malchijah	13th	Huppah	21st	Jachin
6th	Mijamin	14th	Jeshebeab	22nd	Gamul
7th	Hakkoz	15th	Bilgah	23rd	Delaiah
8th	Abijah	16th	Immer	24th	Maaziah

Here were twenty-four households, and between them of those that could perform the duties in the priests' office were thirty-eight thousand. Waiting for ones' lot meant the Levites considered it a privileged time, to be able to serve in the temple. Bear in mind that a priest could only serve in the temple at or after thirty years of age; the opportunity would come around maybe once in the lifetime of those waiting for their lot. Performing tasks such as offering incense, was done only once by a priest, allowing for others to move up on the list, to have the opportunity of offering incense also.

The priests were therefore very careful to marry within their own tribe so as not to corrupt their lineage, keeping it pure and without mixture, thereby maintaining the dignity of the priesthood and their fathers' house, so that the lot to execute the office of the priesthood would not be taken from them. It is recorded that Zachariah and his wife Elisabeth were righteous, they were both Levites and Zachariah's lot had arrived therefore he was in the place about to offer incense to God.

Zachariah as righteous as he was, had a challenge; for both he and Elisabeth were now old and stricken in years, but they were childless. They had prayed and had waited; and were now only holding to the story of their fore-father and his wife, Abraham and Sarah.

Angelic Visitation

While performing his allotted task, Zachariah was greeted by an angel of the Lord, of course, with man's first reaction to the unknown being fear, the angel of the Lord assured Zachariah to not be afraid. The angel then informed him that his prayers had been heard and that Elisabeth would have a son. The angel also instructed Zachariah that the child's name should be called John. Further instructions pertaining to John were:

1. There would be joy and gladness to his parents
2. Many would rejoice because of John's birth
3. He would be great in the sight of the Lord
4. He should neither drink wine nor strong drink
5. He would be filled with the Holy Spirit from his mothers' womb
6. He would turn many of the children of Israel to the Lord
7. God would go before him in the Spirit and power of Elijah
   a. to turn the fathers' heart to their children

b.   and the disobedient to the wisdom of the just

c.   to make ready a people prepared for the Lord

Now, after such a greeting, you may ask how can a righteous man who had been praying for a child, then turn around and question the Lord. Well through sheer shock and fear. Remember, Zachariah was in the temple offering incense. They knew that the presence of God dwelt there and that no one could go into the temple not being of the correct lineage. Furthermore, it was known that if they did not operate as God intended, they could be struck down in the presence of God. Also, bear in mind that the offering of incense was done only once in a priests' lifetime, Zachariah's first thought could have been, my Lord, I am dead, what did I do wrong! After the reassurance from the angel that he should not fear, then hearing all the things that his yet unborn son would accomplish before God, Zachariah's next thought could have been, we (he and Elisabeth) are not worthy. Little me! Why would God choose to use me in this way? Then came the unbelief so he asked for a sign. Now, I cannot say why his asking for a sign was not taken very well that day, for Gideon in the book of Judges asked for a sign when he was visited by an angel.

Jdg 6:16   And the LORD said unto him, Surely I will be with thee, and thou shalt smite the Midianites as one man.

Jdg 6:17   And he said unto him, If now I have found grace in thy sight, then shew me a sign that thou talkest with me.

Gideon's request was honoured, but not Zachariah's. I imagine, that being in the presence of God, offering incense (prayers) would be a time that one would be exhibiting much faith. Please allow me to use my lofty imagination as I liken this to when we come to God, in church, praying, yet we don't believe. How many times have we gotten dressed, gone to the house of God, offered praises, gave thanks, offered up worship and made our requests known unto God. Then when God answers our prayers, we don't believe. How many times have you heard a fellow believer testifying about something they had been praying for, and saying, after it happened "I can't believe it"? This is not pleasing to God. For whether we are in shock or stunned, when God shows up with answers to our prayers, we should give thanks, give praise, give worship, but maintain our faith.

Because of unbelief, Zachariah was struck dumb and had to go through the entire pregnancy with Elisabeth, unable to speak. John the Baptist's birth was announced by Gabriel and in the appointed time, John the Baptist was born.

John's Preparation

At his birth, his father Zachariah was described in the scriptures as also being filled with the Holy Ghost and he prophesied into the life of his son, verses 68-79 of St. Luke chapter 1 records the prophecy of Zachariah over the life of his child John the Baptist. Verse 76 states:

> Luke 1: 76   And thou, child, shalt be called the prophet of the
> Highest: for thou shalt go before the face of the
> Lord to prepare his ways;

Verse 80 of the same chapter declares that John grew and waxed strong in spirit and was in the desert till the day of his showing unto Israel. John the Baptist was called into the wilderness, to live a life of seclusion, isolation and dedication to God. The scripture records that his attire was skin from animals and for food he had a delicacy of locusts and wild honey.

> *Mat 3:4*   *And the same John had his raiment of camel's hair,*
> *and a leathern girdle about his loins; and his meat*
> *was locusts and wild honey.*
>
> *Mar 1:6*   *And John was clothed with camel's hair, and with a*
> *girdle of a skin about his loins; and he did eat locusts*
> *and wild honey;*

The gospels of St. Matthew chapter 3:4 and Mark 1:6 gives us little detail of John's habits in the wilderness, before he bursts on the scene in Luke chapter 3 preaching repentance and baptism (remission of sins) and openly condemning all immorality. John implored those hearing him to repent. The first preacher of repentance and remission of sins via baptism, John spoke a message not heard before.

John the Baptist must have possessed an unshakeable assurance of who he was and what he was called to do. For when he surfaced from the wilderness, he did not conform to the customs or teachings around him. For though there were Pharisees, Sadducees and Scribes, keeping and teaching the things pertaining to the Sabbath and the Law, John the Baptist was not moved or troubled by their customs, as he came on the scene and preached another doctrine.

He knew his purpose and his ministry and was able to answer all those who questioned his identity. The scripture records in several instances where John was question as to whether or not he was the coming Messiah?

> *Joh 1:19*   *And this is the record of John, when the Jews*
> *sent priests and Levites from Jerusalem to ask him,*

Who art thou?

Joh 1:20   *And he confessed, and denied not; but confessed, I am not the Christ.*

Joh 1:21   *And they asked him, What then? Art thou Elias? And he saith, I am not. Art thou that prophet? And he answered, No.*

Joh 1:22   *Then said they unto him, Who art thou? that we may give an answer to them that sent us. What sayest thou of thyself?*

Like John the Baptist, it is imperative for you to know who you are! The devil or the world will always require you to say who you are, and if you are not sure who you are, you could lose your identity and become confused, trying to be someone you are not, or trying to be who they say you are.

I love John the Baptists' answers, first he showed the world that they cannot tell him who he is, John declared, I am NOT the Christ, I am NOT Elias, I am NOT that prophet (who is to come). Every identity they tried to put on John the Baptist was rejected, for he knew who he was. Not only was he able to disallow the identity being placed on him by the world, but he could affirm who he was. He said I am the voice of one crying in the wilderness. John not only knew who he was, but where his ministry would begin and what he was to do.

Joh 1:23   *He said, I am the voice of one crying in the wilderness, Make straight the way of the Lord, as said the prophet Esaias.*

Joh 1:24   *And they which were sent were of the Pharisees.*

Joh 1:25   *And they asked him, and said unto him, Why baptizest thou then, if thou be not that Christ, nor Elias, neither that prophet?*

Joh 1:26	*John answered them, saying, I baptize with water: but there standeth one among you, whom ye know not;*
Joh 1:27	*He it is, who coming after me is preferred before me, whose shoe's latchet I am not worthy to unloose.*
Joh 1:28	*These things were done in Bethabara beyond Jordan, where John was baptizing.*

John knew his role; he described himself as "the voice" of one crying in the wilderness, prepare ye the way of the Lord. He often spoke of the one who would come after him, who was preferred before him. He made reference of this person that he (John) was not even worthy to untie the latchet of his shoes. John was careful to make a clear distinction between him and Jesus Christ, not wanting anyone to mistake him for the Anointed Messiah. John stayed true to his call, his purpose and his ministry. He stated that he (John) baptised with water, but the one after him would baptise with fire.

John had embraced his wilderness experience and allowed God to shape his heart and his purpose. John was the fore-runner of Jesus Christ, he was chosen to baptise the Lord Jesus, it was an act that was included in those which must be fulfilled by Jesus Christ. John's mission was too great for God to allow John to fail. So God kept John in the wilderness long enough, humbling him and drawing him close to himself proving him. God knew that John would stay true to him (God) knowing what was in John's heart, his mission.

God could not take chances with this mission, the fore-runner had to be schooled in the wilderness to learn about himself so that when he started his ministry, he would not lose focus. He knew what was required of him.

Have we been through enough wilderness experiences to allow us to stay true to our calling? For many times those who were called to be one thing, end up doing something else. Sometimes, we receive a compliment and then we get heady and high-minded, running off to operate in that thing. Like John the Baptist, we must learn not to be swayed by what is going on around us. We must stay focused on our purpose. Like John the Baptist, we too must learn to embrace our wilderness experiences and glean from them everything that God is teaching us about: (1) Him (2) about ourselves (3) about our mission and (4) about what is in our heart.

Was John's focus birthed out of the time John stayed in the wilderness? I believe that it was. For you can always pick out those who have been "somewhere" or through "something" with God. Their worship is not pumped or lead, it flows freely; those who know that God had to bring them through a severe test, and had it not been for God, they would have lost their minds. When you have been in harsh wilderness experiences out of which God has brought you, you have a more focused and determined mind to carry on serving him. You look at where you have been and know with full assurance that if God brought you through the things you came through, then he can surely bring you through anything. You are not careful to worship, you are not careful to pray, you are not cute about giving unto God what is due unto him, no matter where you are, for you know that it was God and only God who kept you through your wilderness experience. It was God who provided for you, even if it was locusts and wild honey, he still is a provider.

During the time of John's ministry, Israel was under Roman captivity, with Herod the great reigning as king in Jerusalem from 37BC-4AD.

[Please note: Herod means—king of the Jews, so those in the Roman Senate who ruled over the Jews were called "Herod". Herod is not their names but rather the title given] In the encounter with Jesus in Pilate's quarters when he asked him "Are you the King of the Jews? He was inadvertently asking Jesus, Are you "Herod"? Hence Jesus' response, you have said that I am the King of the Jews. So the sign above Jesus' head on the cross was supposedly a mockery, yet unknown to them, in the mockery, they were declaring what really was true.

The Rulers of John's Day

[28]Augustus Caesar was the Roman Emperor for Jerusalem from around 31BC-14AD, in Galilee, Herod Antipas ruled, Tiberius Caesar was Emperor from AD14-37, and Pontius Pilate was procurator of Judea AD26-36. Israel was expecting a Messiah to come and save them from Roman rule and the war that was at that time being fought between the Romans and the Jews. For anyone caught opposing Roman legislation would be dealt with severely. However, what they looked for did not match up to what they received when the "Messiah" finally appeared on the scene. Sadly, they did not receive or believe him to be the Messiah for whom they waited. Much to their dismay, he was not fighting or leading a revolt against Rome. Instead he taught messages such as love your enemies, do good to them that hate you and rejoice when you are persecuted. I believe those gathered in the courtyard on the day when Jesus was before Pilate and stood sharing the possibility of release with Barabbas, were those who followed politics and was hoping that the Messiah would have aided in and supported their cause; fighting against Roman rule. However, I believe that

---

[28] The New King James Nelson Study Bible

similarly to how many Christians are today, they do not get involved with economic or political issues set up to govern their lives, so too in Jesus' time. Therefore, I strongly believe that those who voted against Jesus and shouted for his imminent crucifixion, were not necessarily the same people Jesus had previously healed and won during his ministry.

John the Baptist's ministry lasted roughly about two years, from AD25-27. Appearing in the dress of camel's hair and leather belt as that of Elijah and operating in the office of a forerunner as did Elijah, John the Baptist understood his ministry to be one of reform and preparation. Calling people from their comfortable homes out into the wilderness to hear the word of God, for during the days of Moses, the wilderness had been a place of righteousness and hope for God's people. John carried the burden of knowing that God was about to do something great, for which the people were not prepared. Just as God tried to prepare Israel for the Promised Land by taking them through the wilderness, so too John the Baptist was trying to get the Jews to be prepared for the coming Messiah. Preaching unto them repentance through baptism and calling them back to the things of the Law, John was very vocal about every kind of immorality that persisted regardless of who the perpetrators were. John was distinctive in who he was, preaching repentance and declaring that he was the "voice of one crying in the wilderness"

Luk 3:3　And he came into all the country about Jordan, preaching the baptism of repentance for the remission of sins;

Luk 3:4　As it is written in the book of the words of Esaias the prophet, saying, The voice of one crying in the wilderness, Prepare ye the way of the Lord, make his paths straight.

Luk 3:5   Every valley shall be filled, and every mountain and hill shall be brought low; and the crooked shall be made straight, and the rough ways *shall be* made smooth;

Luk 3:6   And all flesh shall see the salvation of God.

John preached, giving directives or rebuking specific sect: for he said to the multitude who came to be baptised;

Luk 3:7   *. . . . O generation of vipers, who hath warned you to flee from the wrath to come?*

Luk 3:8   *Bring forth therefore fruits worthy of repentance, and begin not to say within yourselves, We have Abraham to our father: for I say unto you, That God is able of these stones to raise up children unto Abraham.*

Luk 3:9   *And now also the axe is laid unto the root of the trees: every tree therefore which bringeth not forth good fruit is hewn down, and cast into the fire.*

Luk 3:10   *And the people asked him, saying, What shall we do then?*

Luk 3:11   *He answereth and saith unto them, He that hath two coats, let him impart to him that hath none; and he that hath meat, let him do likewise.*

To the publicans who also came to be baptised John said:

Luk 3:13   *. . . . Exact no more than that which is appointed you.*

John addressed the soldiers by saying

Luk 3:14   *. . . . Do violence to no man, neither accuse any falsely; and be content with your wages.*

The people were obviously convicted by the words of John, which indicated that he was a true prophet and one whom they respected and maybe even feared as a man of God, for no one dare answered what he had directed, but took their instruction and got baptised. When the people wondered about who John was in their hearts, John was able to address what they had not said but rather what they were thinking, explaining to them once more that he was not the Christ.

> Luk 3:15   *And as the people were in expectation, and all men mused in their hearts of John, whether he were the Christ, or not;*
>
> Luk 3:16   *John answered, saying unto them all, I indeed baptize you with water; but one mightier than I cometh, the latchet of whose shoes I am not worthy to unloose: he shall baptize you with the Holy Ghost and with fire:*
>
> Luk 3:17   *Whose fan is in his hand, and he will throughly purge his floor, and will gather the wheat into his garner; but the chaff he will burn with fire unquenchable.*
>
> Luk 3:18   *And many other things in his exhortation preached he unto the people.*

But when you preach against immorality, you will always upset some folk. Those who were upset by John the Baptist were of Herod's company.

John's Arrest

John's arrest was birthed out of the fact that he had upset Herodias who was married to Herod Phillip, one of Herod's two sons, (Herod Phillip and Herod Antipas). [29]Antipas was a son of Herod the Great, who had become king of Judea, and Malthace, who was from Samaria. His date of birth is unknown but was before 20 BCE. Antipas, his full brother Archelaus and his half-brother Philip were educated in Rome.

Antipas was not Herod's first choice of heir. That honour fell to Aristobulus and Alexander, Herod's sons by the Hasmonean princess Mariamne. It was only after they were executed (*c.7* BCE), and Herod's oldest son Antipater was convicted of trying to poison his father (5 BCE), that the now elderly Herod fell back on his youngest son Antipas, revising his will to make him heir. During his fatal illness in 4BC, Herod had yet another change of heart about the succession. According to the final version of his will, Antipas' elder brother Archelaus was now to become king of Judea, Idumea and Samaria, while Antipas would rule Galilee and Perea with the lesser title of tetrarch *(Tetrarch—A Roman governor of the fourth part of a province; hence, any subordinate or dependent prince; also, a petty king or sovereign).* Philip was to receive Gaulanitis (the Golan Heights), Batanaea (southern Syria), Trachonitis and Auranitis (Hauran).[5]

Because of Judea's status as a Roman client kingdom, Herod's plans for the succession had to be ratified by Augustus. The three heirs therefore travelled to Rome to make their claims, Antipas arguing he ought to inherit the whole kingdom and the others maintaining that Herod's final will ought to be honoured. Despite qualified support for Antipas from Herodian family

---

[29] *http://en.wikipedia.org/wiki/Herod_Antipas*

members in Rome, who favoured direct Roman rule of Judea but considered Antipas preferable to his brother, Augustus largely confirmed the division of territory set out by Herod in his final will. Archelaus had, however, to be content with the title of ethnarch (*The ruler of a province or a people.*) rather than king.

Early in his reign, Antipas had married the daughter of king Aretas IV of Nabatea. However, while staying in Rome in order to secure the territory of his recently deceased half-brother Herod Philip II (c. AD 34), he fell in love with his brother's widow Herodias (grand-daughter of Herod the Great and Mariamne I), and the two agreed to marry each other, after Herod Antipas had divorced his wife. On learning of this, Aretas' daughter travelled to the fortress of Machaerus, from where Nabatean forces escorted her to her father. Relations between Antipas and Aretas soured and in time preparations began for war. The marriage of Antipas and Herodias took place sometime in AD 34.

Antipas faced more immediate problems in his own tetrarchy after John the Baptist in 28/29 AD according to the Gospel of Luke, began a ministry of preaching and baptism by the Jordan River, which marked the western edge of Antipas' territory of Perea. The New Testament Gospels state that John attacked the tetrarch's marriage as contrary to Jewish law. Herodias was not happy and Herod demanded that John the Baptist be arrested and cast into prison, for what he preached.

> Luk 3:19   *But Herod the tetrarch, being reproved by him for Herodias his brother Philip's wife, and for all the evils which Herod had done,*

Luk 3:20   *Added yet this above all, that he shut up John in*
             prison.

John's Death

The Bible records in St. Mark 6:14-27 the account of John the Baptists' death. After being arrested, Herodias was not happy that John was still alive, she was not happy that one man could have caused such uproar. For those who were not aware of what had happened, now knew of her adulterous relationship with Herod Antipas, because of John's public speaking. Though it was Herod Antipas' decision to divorce Aretas' daughter which broke down relations between Antipas and Aretas and caused preparations for war to begin, Herodias and Herod were looking for someone to blame. John the Baptist was not helping the situation when he condemned their actions. If the war began, the people would blame them for causing it and they might not have the support of those in the tetrarchy. Therefore, Herodias desiring to have John killed, took advantage of the opportunity given of Herod to her daughter Salome at dinner when she danced, that he would have given her anything within the kingdom that she required. This statement coupled with her knowledge that Herod Antipas was trying desperately to impress those who sat at meat with him, Herodias then made her move.

Salome went to her mother for advice as to what she (Salome) should request, Herodias wasted no time and instructed her to ask for the head of John the Baptist, and so she (Salome) did.

Herod regretted making such an oath and more so that Salome had made such a request. However, he ordered the beheading of John the Baptist, not because he wanted to kill John the Baptist, but because he wanted those who sat with him, described in St. Mark 6:21 as his lords, high captain and chief estates of Galilee, to see him as a man of his word. He had made an oath, though foolish, to an immature child and she had gone to her scheming mother to ask advice. Her mother's plan was playing out well for now she could have what she always wanted, the death of the prophet John the Baptist, and no one could contest it, because it had been ordered by Herod himself.

> *Mar 6:26* *And the king was exceeding sorry; yet for his oath's sake, and for their sakes which sat with him, he would not reject her.*
>
> *Mar 6:27* *And immediately the king sent an executioner, and commanded his head to be brought: and he went and beheaded him in the prison,*

Was John the Baptist effective and successful in his ministry? Yes he was, he had done exactly what he had been called, appointed and set out to do. To be the voice and prepared the way for the Lord. Though John the Baptists' his ministry only lasted two years, Jesus made reference that among those born of women, there was none greater than John the Baptist. When God himself has such a testimony about you, then that shows that you have done what he required and it is well pleasing unto him.

Questions for Chapter 9:

1. John the Baptist's lineage is mentioned in the scriptures, showing a link to the tribe of the Levites. Conduct an investigation on the lineage of the disciples tracing their lineage to the varying tribes.

2. In no less than 1000 words, give your own account of John the Baptist's reason for questioning whether Jesus was the Messiah, as found in Matthew 11:2-3 and Luke 7:19-20.

Mat 11:2	Now when John had heard in the prison the works of Christ, he sent two of his disciples,
Mat 11:3	And said unto him, Art thou he that should come, or do we look for another?
Luk 7:19	And John calling *unto him* two of his disciples sent *them* to Jesus, saying, Art thou he that should come? or look we for another?
Luk 7:20	When the men were come unto him, they said, John Baptist hath sent us unto thee, saying, Art thou he that should come? or look we for another?

Isaiah 12:2

Behold, God is my salvation; I will trust, and not be afraid: for the LORD JEHOVAH is my strength and my song; he also is become my salvation.

CHAPTER 10

"Wilderness Experience—Jesus"

Starting a chapter to speak about the God of heaven is not as easy as I thought it would be. For how do I explain the beginning of God? He has no beginning and no end. However, I will look at the period when the word was made flesh and dwelt among us.

The Divinity of Jesus Christ

Jesus, the express image (person) of God as described in Hebrews 1:3, whilst here on earth, endured a wilderness experience.

> *Heb 1:3*   *Who being the brightness of his glory, and the express image of his person, and upholding all things by the word of his power, when he had by himself purged our sins, sat down on the right hand of the Majesty on high;*

Hebrews 1:3 means when God expressed himself in an image of human characteristics, that image is Jesus Christ. Why do I say of human characteristics? Because throughout the Old Testament, God has expressed himself in many forms which were not human, forms such as:

- The burning bush (Exodus 3:2-4)

Exo 3:2	And the angel of the LORD appeared unto him in a flame of fire out of the midst of a bush: and he looked, and, behold, the bush burned with fire, and the bush *was* not consumed.
Exo 3:3	And Moses said, I will now turn aside, and see this great sight, why the bush is not burnt.
Exo 3:4	And when the LORD saw that he turned aside to see, God called unto him out of the midst of the bush, and said, Moses, Moses. And he said, Here *am* I.

- The pillar of cloud by day (Exodus 13:21-22)
- The pillar of fire by night (Exodus 13:21-22)

Exo 13:21	And the LORD went before them by day in a pillar of a cloud, to lead them the way; and by night in a pillar of fire, to give them light; to go by day and night:
Exo 13:22	He took not away the pillar of the cloud by day, nor the pillar of fire by night, *from* before the people. To name but a few:

Why Did God Come to Earth?

What was God doing here on earth to have endured a wilderness experience? Before I can look at the actual experience, let me take you back through the corridors of time to when it became necessary for God to manifest himself in flesh, and in a body that could die, so that man could be saved.

The Plan of Salvation

Before God created man, he devised the plan to save man. That is the wisdom of God. The book of Revelation, chapter 13 and verse 8 made reference to the book of life of the Lamb (Jesus Christ) slain from the foundation of the world. Ephesians 1:4 also makes reference to us being chosen in him (Jesus Christ) before the foundation of the world. Before the foundations of the world were laid, God made provision for us in this great salvation. However, though the Lamb was slain long before time was, we had to meet up with the actual manifestation of the work done previously in God's fullness of time. The epistle of Galatians (Gal. 4:4-5) explained this by saying, but when the fullness of the time was come, God sent forth his son, made of a woman, made under the law, to redeem them that were under the law.

However, God gave hints across and through the Old Testament from the writings of Genesis, about the plan he had put in place for us.

Genesis gives the account of when Adam and Eve had disobeyed God and eaten of the tree of the knowledge of good and evil. God turned up and Adam was not in the place (spiritually) where he had previously been. God immediately asked him whether he had eaten of the tree which he had instructed him not to eat. Adam answered yes and God began meting out the punishments which came as a result of disobedience, punishment to the serpent, to the woman and to the man.

> *Gen 3:14   And the LORD God said unto the serpent,*
> *Because thou hast done this, thou art cursed above*
> *all cattle, and above every beast of the field;*
> *upon thy belly shalt thou go, and dust shalt thou*
> *eat all the days of thy life:*

Gen 3:15   *And I will put enmity between thee and the woman, and between thy seed and her seed; it shall bruise thy head, and thou shalt bruise his heel.*

Gen 3:16   *Unto the woman he said, I will greatly multiply thy sorrow and thy conception; in sorrow thou shalt bring forth children; and thy desire shall be to thy husband, and he shall rule over thee.*

Gen 3:17   *And unto Adam he said, Because thou hast hearkened unto the voice of thy wife, and hast eaten of the tree, of which I commanded thee, saying, Thou shalt not eat of it: cursed is the ground for thy sake; in sorrow shalt thou eat of it all the days of thy life;*

Gen 3:18   *Thorns also and thistles shall it bring forth to thee; and thou shalt eat the herb of the field;*

Gen 3:19   *In the sweat of thy face shalt thou eat bread, till thou return unto the ground; for out of it wast thou taken: for dust thou art, and unto dust shalt thou return.*

Please note, verse 15 is not to be missed, as God gave a clue as to what was to come. God said unto the serpent, I will put enmity (hostility/hate) between thee and the woman, and between thy seed and her seed . . . . Stop a minute! A woman does not have a seed, so to what was God referring? The seed of life was and has always been in the man, so when God; who does not make a mistake, or say idle words, refers to "her seed" he indirectly said to the serpent one day, the woman will bring forth without aid of the seed of a man. This seed would also be male and have the ability to bring forth after its kind. For if the ability to bring forth seed, lies with a seed, then that seed, will bring forth after its kind, this is obeying the laws locked into the seed as God has commanded in the creation. Do remember, everything was commanded to bring forth after its kind. This seed would therefore have the ability to do the same. This brought fear to Satan, in so much that he tried to kill the "seed" by killing the first born of Egypt, while they were in Goshen, just as Moses was coming into the world and again killing all the baby boys when Jesus was coming into the world.

Exo 1:15   *And the king of Egypt spake to the Hebrew midwives, of which the name of the one was Shiphrah, and the name of the other Puah:*

Exo 1:16   *And he said, When ye do the office of a midwife to the Hebrew women, and see them upon the stools; if it be a son, then ye shall kill him: but if it be a daughter, then she shall live.*

Mat 2:16   *Then Herod, when he saw that he was mocked of the wise men, was exceeding wroth, and sent forth, and slew all the children that were in Bethlehem, and in all the coasts thereof, from two years old and under, according to the time which he had diligently enquired of the wise men.*

Mat 2:17   *Then was fulfilled that which was spoken by Jeremy the prophet, saying,*

Mat 2:18   *In Rama was there a voice heard, lamentation, and weeping, and great mourning, Rachel weeping for her children, and would not be comforted, because they are not.*

The Ark

Also depicting the plan of salvation was the ark God instructed Noah to build. In Genesis chapter 6, we find Noah being told by God about impending danger, a flood that would wipe out mankind. However, Noah and his house were chosen by God to be saved from this disaster. God told Noah to build an ark of gopher wood. God proceeded to give Noah all the specifications of the ark.

Gen 6:13   *And God said unto Noah, The end of all flesh is come before me; for the earth is filled with violence through them; and, behold, I will destroy them with the earth.*

Gen 6:14   *Make thee an ark of gopher wood; rooms shalt thou make in the ark, and shalt pitch it within and without with pitch.*

Gen 6:15   *And this is the fashion which thou shalt make it of: The length of the ark shall be three hundred cubits, the breadth of it fifty cubits, and the height of it thirty cubits.*

Gen 6:16   *A window shalt thou make to the ark, and in a cubit shalt thou finish it above; and the door of the ark shalt thou set in the side thereof; with lower, second, and third stories shalt thou make it.*

I do feel compelled at this juncture to dispel a myth I have heard repeated so many times. I have always heard it said that Noah preached for 120yrs. I have searched and have now concluded that this is not so. When God called and commissioned Noah to build the ark, his sons Shem, Ham and Japheth were already existed. Genesis 5:32 records that Noah was 500yrs old when he became a father. Genesis 7:6 tells us that Noah was 600yrs old when the flood of waters was upon the earth. So then;

1. *If God called Noah after his sons were born*
2. *Noah began having children when he was 500yrs*
3. *The entering into the ark happened at 600yrs old*
4. *Then the flood preaching could not have been for 120yrs. God had not called Noah to build until after he was 500yrs old.*

Now in Chapter 6 of Genesis, and verse 3, the Bible records God saying that his Spirit would not always strive with men . . . but yet his days shall be 120 yrs. I believe that this 120 is what is being referred to incorrectly where Noah's preaching time is concerned.

If we investigate the scriptures, we will see that prior to the flood, men lived very long lives, in sin. We know from the Genesis account that it was not God's intention originally for man to die, hence the tree of life in the Garden of Eden. However, sin was now passed upon man but God's Spirit was allowing man to live long lives. i.e. Adam 930yrs, Seth lived 912yrs, Cainan lived 910yrs, Mahalaleel 895yrs, Jared 962yrs, to name but a few.

God had to watch man live long lives in sin. By the time we get to Genesis 6, the Bible records that the wickedness of man upon the earth was great, and his thoughts were evil continually. God then made a switch, and after the flood, mans' years were drastically cut. The grace period after the flood for man to live became 120yrs. Slowly man started to die much earlier in life, hence the scripture being fulfilled, that the Spirit of God would no longer strive with man.

I conclude therefore, that Noah did not preach about the flood for 120yrs, but rather a period between 500 (when he was called) and 600 (when he entered into the ark), so really less than 100 years. Also, I conclude that the 120yrs, refer not to Noah's preaching time span, but rather it represents the amount of years God has given us to live. With good health and exercise, today we can still get to 120yrs, but God definitely has placed a cap on the length of time man stays on the earth; definitely evident in mans' length of days prior to the flood and after the flood.

1 Peter 3:20-21draws reference for baptism from the event of the flood. The saving of souls from the flood prefigured the salvation by water baptism. The temporal saving of the eight souls was a type the antitype is the eternal saving of many.

> 1Pe 3:20   *Which sometime were disobedient, when once the longsuffering of God waited in the days of Noah, while the ark was a preparing, wherein few, that is, eight souls were saved by water.*
>
> 1Pe 3:21   *The like figure whereunto even baptism doth also now save us (not the putting away of the filth of the flesh, but the answer of a good conscience toward God,) by the resurrection of Jesus Christ:*

Peter was careful to show that though the actual act is washing of the flesh, the symbolic act bears a much deeper and eternal meaning of the soul that will hold to and maintain the covenant made via baptism.

The Tabernacle

Another clue given in the word of the salvation plan which was set up from before the foundation of the world is depicted in the book of Exodus. This is seen in the actual blueprint of the tabernacle, which God had given to Moses and warned him regarding the specifications; that Moses should ensure it was made just as it had been shown him in the mount.

> Exo 25:9   According to all that I shew thee, *after* the pattern of the tabernacle, and the pattern of all the instruments thereof, even so shall ye make *it*.

The tabernacle and all its components were a depiction of that which was to come, all locked into the plan of salvation.

Heb 8:5   *Who serve unto the example and shadow of heavenly things, as Moses was admonished of God when he was about to make the tabernacle: for, See, saith he, that thou make all things according to the pattern shewed to thee in the mount.*

Col 2:17   *Which are a shadow of things to come; but the body is of Christ.*

The tabernacle was a shadow the very image of that shadow was Jesus Christ.

Heb 9:2   *For there was a tabernacle made; the first, wherein was the candlestick, and the table, and the shewbread; which is called the sanctuary.*

Heb 9:3   *And after the second veil, the tabernacle which is called the Holiest of all;*

Heb 9:4   *Which had the golden censer, and the ark of the covenant overlaid round about with gold, wherein was the golden pot that had manna, and Aaron's rod that budded, and the tables of the covenant;*

Heb 9:5   *And over it the cherubims of glory shadowing the mercyseat; of which we cannot now speak particularly.*

Heb 9:6   *Now when these things were thus ordained, the priests went always into the first tabernacle, accomplishing the service of God.*

Heb 9:7   *But into the second went the high priest alone once every year, not without blood, which he offered for himself, and for the errors of the people:*

The shadow seen in the Old Testament, of the tabernacle was being cast by the very image of Jesus Christ in the New Testament, and the New

Testament image of Jesus Christ, cast a shadow visible as the tabernacle in the Old Testament. If we are to investigate the tabernacle and some of its items, we would see the wisdom and strategic planning of God.

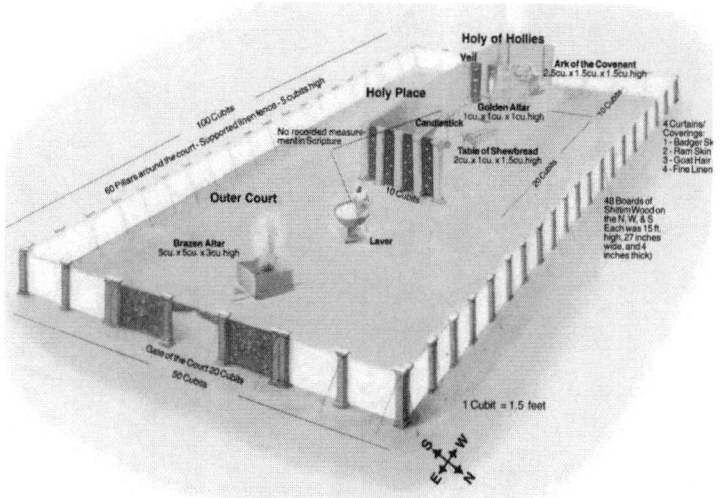

Everything showed the awesome plan of God. For instance, the courtyard of the tabernacle had only one gate. This meant therefore that those approaching God could only approach him as he had set out and not as they pleased. No matter where they camped, (as the very place where each tribe camped was designated), they could not approach from any other area and none had a preferred entrance separated from others. Everyone who approached God, must enter through the same (one) gate. There was only one gate and every man had to come in the same way.

Like the Tabernacle, the Ark built by Noah, also had only one way of entering. The tabernacle had one gate, the ark had one door. This is significant, pointing to Jesus as the only one way to salvation:

Joh 14:6 Jesus saith unto him, I am the way, the truth, and the life: no man cometh unto the Father, but by me.

On entering the courtyard, there would be a brazen altar, where sacrificial offerings were made. The brazen altar was made of wood from acacia tree and then overlaid with bronze, symbolizing judgment for sin. Sinful man cannot approach the holy God without making a sacrifice for his sins.

This meant that an innocent creature would be used to make atonement for his sin. The animal would be taken and the hand of the man would be laid upon the head of the animal, an act which was symbolic of the sin of the man being transferred to the animal. The animal was then sacrificed and that sacrifice was deemed as payment or atonement for the committed sin.

Lev 1:4   *And he shall put his hand upon the head of the burnt offering; and it shall be accepted for him to make atonement for him.*

Lev 1:5   *And he shall kill the bullock before the LORD: and the priests, Aaron's sons, shall bring the blood, and sprinkle the blood round about upon the altar that is by the door of the tabernacle of the congregation.*

Lev 17:11   *For the life of a creature is in the blood, and I have given it to you to make atonement for yourselves on the altar; it is the blood that makes atonement for one's life.*

As soon as man sets out in his mind to approach where God is, they must sacrifice or give up something.

Heb 9:22   *And almost all things are by the law purged with blood; and without shedding of blood is no remission*

The offerings used were many in those days, each bearing specific significance depending on the type of offering.

1. Meat offering (Leviticus 2:12-14)

    a. of fine flour

        i.   this offering was one tenth of fine flour with oil and frankincense, seasoned with salt

    b. of first fruits

                                                                    ii.

2. Drink offering

    this offering was of green ears of corn dried by fire, seasoned with salta.   This was wine, measuring the fourth part of a hin (there are twenty-two references to "hin" made in the scripture. Twelve towards oil, eight towards wine, one to water and one to ephah. Though I have searched and researched, it is not sure what equates to the measurement of "hin").

3. Sin offering / Trespass offering

    a. For the priest: a young bullock without blemish, with

the fat of the inwards removed; also its' flesh, skin and dung was removed and burned outside the camp. The priest would dip his finger in the blood and place it on the horns of the brazen altar and the rest would be poured out by the altar.b.   For the people: bullock without blemish; or if the sin was known, then a male or female kid without blemish, if the sin was unknown, then a female lamb without blemish, if they could not afford the lamb, then two turtledoves or two young pigeons, if that could not be afforded, then one tenth part of an ephah of fine flour, with no oil or frankincense. (Lev. 4:3-20, 4:28, 32, 5:11)

4.   Offering of atonement: similar to the animals offered for the sin offering but offered once a year by the priest. This time the blood was not poured out at the altar, but rather taken with the priest into the tabernacle. He had to then wash, enter into the tabernacle, change his clothes bathe himself and put on the holy garments, which were white. Carrying the blood of the bullock, the priest would dip his finger in the blood, place it on the horns of the altar and sprinkle blood seven times before the Lord, even before the veil of the sanctuary. The blood was also sprinkled upon and before the mercy seat (Leviticus 16:16-34)

5.   Peace offering: this was a male or female kid without blemish with the fat covering the inwards removed (Lev 3:1)

6.   Thanksgiving offering: this was unleavened cakes with oil,

wafers with oil and cake with oil of fine flour, fried. (Lev 7:2)

7. Heave offering: this was one of the oblations offered for thanksgiving, given to the priest.

Jesus took our place as the spotless lamb, slain from the foundation of the world. All these offerings which were necessary have now been replaced. Jesus has become our peace, he became sin for us. Now whilst we are not baking cakes to offer to the priest, we now bring a monetary offering to enable the house of God to always have "meat" Malachi 3:10.

> Mal 3:10   *Bring ye all the tithes into the storehouse, that there may be meat in mine house, and prove me now herewith, saith the LORD of hosts, if I will not open you the windows of heaven, and pour you out a blessing, that there shall not be room enough to receive it.*

The spotless lamb or lamb without blemish is significant of Jesus Christ, as he committed no sin, and unlike us, he was not born in sin. He was deemed spotless and without blemish.

> 2Co 5:21   *For he hath made him to be sin for us, who knew no sin; that we might be made the righteousness of God in him.*
>
> 1Pe 2:22   *Who did no sin, neither was guile found in his mouth:*
>
> 1Jn 3:5   *And ye know that he was manifested to take away our sins; and in him is no sin.*

Those who practiced offering bullocks, turtledoves, young pigeons, lambs, male and female goats were doing what was necessary for their sins to be rolled back for a year. For they would have to perform these sacrificial rituals yearly to ensure that they were pronounced forgiven. However, that forgiveness only lasted for a year, and even less if they had sinned before the next atonement offering. But thanks be to God, when Jesus entered into the most holy place in heaven to offer his blood, it was required only once.

> *Heb 9:13*   *For if the blood of bulls and of goats, and the ashes of an heifer sprinkling the unclean, sanctifieth to the purifying of the flesh:*
>
> *Heb 9:14*   *How much more shall the blood of Christ, who through the eternal Spirit offered himself without spot to God, purge your conscience from dead works to serve the living God?*

He went in as the High priest, carrying his own blood as the Lamb, and his blood allowed for the continual forgiveness of sin.

> *Heb 9:11*   *But Christ being come an high priest of good things to come, by a greater and more perfect tabernacle, not made with hands, that is to say, not of this building;*
>
> *Heb 9:12*   *Neither by the blood of goats and calves, but by his own blood he entered in once into the holy place, having obtained eternal redemption for us.*

Do remember, God had set this symbolic event up long before Christ walked the earth. God gave so many clues in his word to show us that he had truly predestined us.

Let's look at another article in the tabernacle, the Menorah or golden candlestick. The candlestick stood on the left side of the holy place. It was made out of one piece of pure gold.

It had a central branch from which three branches extended on either side. Forming a total of seven branches, each branch was used to hold olive oil with wicks coming from each. Similar to that of an almond tree, each side contained buds, blossoms and flowers. The candlestick was to always have fire burning continuously. Aaron was to tend the menorah ensuring it had enough oil and that the wick was sufficient, both morning and evening. Burning continuously, the menorah was the only source of light in the tabernacle.

The Menorah is significant to Jesus he is the light of the world, the only source of light for man in a dark world. Without Jesus, men walk around in the dark. Just as without the menorah the priest would be moping around in the dark so it is for anyone who lives without Jesus today.

> Joh 1:4   *In him was life; and the life was the light of men.*
>
> Joh 1:5   *And the light shineth in darkness; and the darkness comprehended it not.*
>
> Joh 8:12   *Then spake Jesus again unto them, saying, I am the light of the world: he that followeth me shall not walk in darkness, but shall have the light of life.*
>
> Joh 9:5   *As long as I am in the world, I am the light of the world.*

Everything within the tabernacle pointed to Jesus Christ.

The reason for the sanctuary or tabernacle was so that God would be able to dwell among the children of Israel. Now the fact that God is omnipresent with nowhere hid from him and with us even living in him, why would he be so adamant to "dwell among men". This I believe was another clue of that which was to come.

> *Exo 25:8*   *And let them make me a sanctuary; that I may dwell among them.*

This pointed to the infilling of the Holy Ghost which was God dwelling in man. However, the clues God gave were given to his prophets and to those whom he chose to reveal them. For God had shrouded the plan of salvation in a mystery and hid the church, allowing portions of revelations to such prophets as Isaiah, Zachariah, Joel, David and a few others. They spoke of things they were not even sure of themselves and did not even live to see, but God allowed them to prophesy of things that were to come. Moses built the tabernacle as he had seen the pattern shown by God in the mountain, but had no idea the significance it would have thousands of years of later.

> *1Co 2:7*   *But we speak the wisdom of God in a mystery, even the hidden wisdom, which God ordained before the world unto our glory:*
>
> *1Co 2:8*   *Which none of the princes of this world knew: for had they known it, they would not have crucified the Lord of glory.*

If Satan had known the impact of shedding the blood of Jesus Christ, he would never have him crucified. The actual act of the crucifixion was settled and done from before the foundations of the world, but manifested over two thousand years ago. The plan of salvation was set in place ready for the fall of man.

The Creation

Firstly, we must realise that there is nothing that man has that God needs. I point this out as a few months ago whilst in discussion with an atheist, his understanding was that a God, who created man to fellowship with, was in need of something and if he is in need of something then he cannot be God. Well, I believe and know of a fact that God does not need man, but rather man needs God. God existed long before the creation of man. God made a being (man) and decided to impart to that being a piece of himself. When God blew into man's nostrils the breath of life, God gave man intelligence, logic, will, emotions, he made man cognitive, allowing man the ability to reason and process thinking through intuition and perception. He caused man to be able to think.

God also imparts into man, something that was not of man, (man's spirit) so that man would need to go back to the source to gain more, much like a drug; man needed now to fellowship with the being higher than itself. Remember, man was made from dust, minerals of all sorts were in the makeup of man, but without the breath of God, man was a clay image, without life, with no thinking power or life-like ability. When God breathed into man and made him a living "Nephus" (soul) that soul became a spiritual being living inside of a clay shell, allowing the processing of thoughts, creating image through imagination, possessing intuition, intelligence, perception and now being aware. Aware of:

1. Another being higher than himself

2. His surroundings

3. His conscious state

4. His emotions, &

5. Others

Man became aware of a higher being, man knows he did not create himself, and this knowledge is innate. With this innate knowledge then comes the need to worship. Every man (mankind/human kind/both male and female) has within him the need to worship something or someone and man will worship that thing; in search, without even realising it, of that higher being.

Some worship:
1. Themselves

2. Sports

3. Things (cars/ houses/kingdoms)

4. Fame/prosperity

5. Heroes (celebrities/etc.)

6. Idols

7. The One True and Living God

However, man was created without sin, and this sinless state allowed man to have fellowship with God. The scripture shows that Adam's fellowship with God was so great that God allowed him to even name each beast of the garden; such oneness with God that Adam could even tap into God's thought and come up with the designated name for each animal, as was meant by God.

> Gen 2:19   And out of the ground the LORD God formed every beast of the field, and every fowl of the air; and brought them unto Adam to see what he would call them: and

whatsoever Adam called every living creature,
that *was* the name thereof.

Gen 2:20   And Adam gave names to all cattle, and to the
fowl of the air, and to every beast of the field
. . .

This fellowship did not exist because God needed to fellowship with man, but rather because man needed to stay close to God in fellowship; as God is the source from which the life of man emits. Without the fellowship with God, man's purpose in existence is lost. God however, cannot fellowship with man if man is in sin, therefore, man needed to remain in a sinless state for fellowship with God to continue.

The Fall of Man

At the beginning of the scriptures, the book of Genesis gives account of the fall of man, a fall which plunged mankind into a sinful abyss. Man had disobeyed the one instruction given them by God, not to eat of the tree of the knowledge of good and evil which was in the midst of the garden of Eden (Genesis 2:15-17).

Gen 2:15   And the LORD God took the man, and put
him into the garden of Eden to dress it and to
keep it.

Gen 2:16   And the LORD God commanded the man,
saying, Of every tree of the garden thou
mayest freely eat:

Gen 2:17   But of the tree of the knowledge of good and
evil, thou shalt not eat of it: for in the day
that thou eatest thereof thou shalt surely die.

Through man's disobedience, his dominion over the earth was

handed to the devil as man was introduced to sin through disobedience, causing sin to be passed down through the generations of mankind.

> Rom 5:12   Wherefore, as by one man sin entered into the world, and death by sin; and so death passed upon all men, for that all have sinned:

Man's fall separated man from God, thereby severing the cords of fellowship from God, for God cannot fellowship with sinful man, again, not for God's sake, but for man's sake, as man would be consumed in the presence of God, because of sin.

The wonderful thing with God is that he knows all things, he is omniscient (Omni meaning all and science meaning knowledge). God has all knowledge and this knowledge transcends time. God sees and knows the past, present and future all at once, separating the end from the beginning. Therefore, God knew that man would fall into sin and that if left in that sinful state, man would self-destruct. Therefore, before man was even created, God had orchestrated a plan to save man from sin and from himself.

God knew that man would have fallen into sin, before he created him. God knew that man would not have pleased him, God knew man was frail and weak and unable to live a life free from sin. God knew man, his prize creation, would have caused him much grief and even regret, yet, because of his love for man, God made provisions before he made man, to save man.

After the naming of the animals, the Bible records that God

concluded that it was not good for man to be alone, for until that time, there was no mate found for Adam. God decided to separate a part of man from himself, in order that procreation could take place. This meant therefore, that man would have to go back to get that part of himself in order to reproduce.

The Bible states that God caused a deep sleep to fall upon Adam and whilst Adam was sleeping, God performed surgery on Adam. He took one of Adam's rib, and from it he made a woman. Adam named her Eve.

Prior to Eve being formed, God had instructed Adam what to eat and what not to eat. I can assume that Adam would at some point have passed this instruction on to Eve, whether out of just making her aware; or Eve could have observed that Adam did not eat from that particular tree, in the midst of the garden. Let me at this juncture remind you of James' explanation of how temptation occurs: In James chapter 1:14, James explains that *"every man is tempted when he is drawn away of his own lust"* so Eve's temptation regarding the tree of the knowledge of good and evil could have come about only because she was "drawn away", be it out of curiosity or wanting to simply taste the fruit of that tree. For whatever the reason, Eve was enticed and so it became the devil's playground.

For when that "lust" hath conceived, meaning when you give in to the thing by which you are tempted, then it brings forth sin (James 1:15).

Jas 1:14	*But every man is tempted, when he is drawn away of his own lust, and enticed.*
Jas 1:15	*Then when lust hath conceived, it bringeth forth sin: and sin, when it is finished, bringeth forth death.*

Eve's Encounter with the Serpent

Satan recognised that Eve had a "lusting" toward the tree which he knew she was not to eat from. Bear in mind, we do not know how long Adam and Eve were on the earth before they sinned. We do know however that Cain and Abel were not yet born. Satan struck up a conversation with Eve and in that conversation convinced her to eat of something God had given strict instruction not to eat. Then Eve gave it to Adam and then, mankind was corrupted. Notice, the seed of man is in the man. Eve's eating had only brought sin upon Eve, Adam's eating brought sin upon all of mankind; because the seed was in Adam and a polluted Adam, meant a polluted mankind.

Rom 5:12	*Wherefore, as by one man sin entered into the world, and death by sin; and so death passed upon all men, for that all have sinned:*

This act of eating of the fruit of the tree of knowledge of good and evil by Adam brought about the necessity of the implementation of the plan which had been made by God.

The Birth of Jesus Christ

> Gal 4:4   But when the fulness of the time was come,
> God sent forth his Son, made of a woman,
> made under the law,

The scripture is evident that God had locked in time when he would reveal the plan of salvation. It is evident also that he had chosen the specific time, dispensation, culture, political rule, date, time and place for this plan to be implemented. Isaiah had prophesied hundreds of years prior that a virgin would be with child, many must have thought him crazy for the very nature of reproduction required that procreation has taken place. Isaiah also prophesied that the child would be called, God with us or Emmanuel. Many prophecies were made concerning the arrival of the anointed one, Jesus Christ. Some of those prophecies and their fulfillments are as follows:

Prophecy	Fulfillment
Subject: Seed of the Woman	
Gen 3:15 And I will put enmity between thee and the woman, and between thy seed and her seed, it shall bruise thy head, and thou shalt bruise his heel.	Gal. 4:4 But when the fulness of the time was come, God sent forth his Son, made of a woman, made under the law
Subject: Descendant of Abraham	
Gen 12:3 And I will bless them that bless thee, and curse him that curseth thee: and in thee shall all families of the earth be blessed	Matt 1:1 The book of the generation of Jesus Christ, the son of David, the son of Abraham
Subject: Descendant of Isaac	
Gen 17:19 And God said, Sarah thy wife shall bear thee a son indeed; and thou shalt call his name Isaac: and I will establish my covenant with him for an everlasting covenant, *and* with his seed after him	Luke 3:34 Which was *the son* of Jacob, which was *the son* of Isaac, which was *the son* of Abraham, which was *the son* of Thara, which was *the son* of Nachor

Subject: Descendant of Jacob	
Num 24:17 I shall see him, but not now: I shall behold him, but not nigh: there shall come a Star out of Jacob, and a Sceptre shall rise out of Israel, and shall smite the corners of Moab, and destroy all the children of Sheth.	Matt 1:2 Abraham begat Isaac; and Isaac begat Jacob; and Jacob begat Judas and his brethren;
Subject: Tribe of Judah	
Gen 49:10 The sceptre shall not depart from Judah, nor a lawgiver from between his feet, until Shiloh come; and unto him *shall* the gathering of the people *be.*	Luke 3:33 Which was *the son* of Aminadab, which was *the son* of Aram, which was *the son* of Esrom, which was *the son* of Phares, which was *the son* of Juda,
Subject: Heir to David's throne	
Is 9:7 Of the increase of *his* government and peace *there shall be* no end, upon the throne of David, and upon his kingdom, to order it, and to establish it with judgment and with justice from henceforth even for ever. The zeal of the LORD of hosts will perform this.	Luke 1:32-33 A light to lighten the Gentiles, and the glory of thy people Israel. And Joseph and his mother marvelled at those things which were spoken of him.
Mic 5:2 But thou, Bethlehem Ephratah, *though* thou be little among the thousands of Judah, *yet* out of thee shall he come forth unto me *that is* to be ruler in Israel; whose goings forth *have been* from of old, from everlasting.	Luke 2:4-5, 7 And Joseph also went up from Galilee, out of the city of Nazareth, into Judaea, unto the city of David, which is called Bethlehem; (because he was of the house and lineage of David:) To be taxed with Mary his espoused wife, being great with child. And so it was, that, while they were there, the days were accomplished that she should be delivered. And she brought forth her firstborn son, and wrapped him in swaddling clothes, and laid him in a manger; because there was no room for them in the inn.
Subject: Born of a virgin	
Isa 7:14 Therefore the Lord himself shall give you a sign; Behold, a virgin shall	Luke 1:26-27 &30-31 And in the sixth month the angel

134

conceive, and bear a son, and shall call his name Immanuel.	Gabriel was sent from God unto a city of Galilee, named Nazareth, To a virgin espoused to a man whose name was Joseph, of the house of David; and the virgin's name *was* Mary. And the angel said unto her, Fear not, Mary: for thou hast found favour with God. And, behold, thou shalt conceive in thy womb, and bring forth a son, and shalt call his name JESUS.
Slaughter of children	
Jer 31:15 Thus saith the LORD; A voice was heard in Ramah, lamentation, *and* bitter weeping; Rahel weeping for her children refused to be comforted for her children, because they *were* not	Matt 2:16-18 Then Herod, when he saw that he was mocked of the wise men, was exceeding wroth, and sent forth, and slew all the children that were in Bethlehem, and in all the coasts thereof, from two years old and under, according to the time which he had diligently enquired of the wise men. Then was fulfilled that which was spoken by Jeremy the prophet, saying, In Rama was there a voice heard, lamentation, and weeping, and great mourning, Rachel weeping *for* her children, and would not be comforted, because they are not

The prophets were given a glimpse into the coming of Jesus Christ. The time was set; the scene was as it was ordained by God. With all the players in place, God enrobed himself in flesh, taking on the likeness of flesh, to redeem us.

1 Tim 3:16 And without controversy great is the mystery of godliness: God was manifest in the flesh, justified in the Spirit, seen of angels, preached unto the Gentiles, believed on in the world, received up into glory.

Jesus' Life & Wilderness Experience

Having a set focus that there were three and one half years in which his ministry must unfold. During which time, he needed to select and train twelve men as disciples to carry on with the work, Jesus wasted no time. As a child we read about his travel to Jerusalem where he was mistakenly left by Mary and Joseph, and then being found of them in the temple.

Luk 2:40 *And the child grew, and waxed strong in spirit, filled with wisdom: and the grace of God was upon him.*

Luk 2:41 *Now his parents went to Jerusalem every year at the feast of the passover.*

Luk 2:42 *And when he was twelve years old, they went up to Jerusalem after the custom of the feast.*

Luk 2:43 *And when they had fulfilled the days, as they returned, the child Jesus tarried behind in Jerusalem; and Joseph and his mother knew not of it.*

Luk 2:44 *But they, supposing him to have been in the company, went a day's journey; and they sought him among their kinsfolk and acquaintance.*

Luk 2:45 *And when they found him not, they turned back again to Jerusalem, seeking him.*

Luk 2:46 *And it came to pass, that after three days they found him in the temple, sitting in the midst of the doctors, both hearing them, and asking them questions.*

Luk 2:47   *And all that heard him were astonished at his understanding and answers.*

Luk 2:48   *And when they saw him, they were amazed: and his mother said unto him, Son, why hast thou thus dealt with us? behold, thy father and I have sought thee sorrowing.*

Luk 2:49   *And he said unto them, How is it that ye sought me? wist ye not that I must be about my Father's business?*

Though Jesus was yet a child, he knew what he was about. Not much is mentioned in the scriptures, about his life growing up. We see him at birth, we see him at twelve years old in the temple. Then we next see him getting ready to be baptised, after which he started selecting and gathering his disciples, then we see him at a marriage being held at Cana according to the account of St. John. However, if we look at the gospel of Matthew, we see his birth, Matthew does not record the marriage of Cana, but it records something else which is pivotal for my writing. It records the wilderness experience of Jesus.

After Jesus' baptism by John the Baptist, Jesus went into the wilderness. Matthew's account states that he was led of the Spirit, into the wilderness to be tempted of the devil.

Matt 4:1   *Then was Jesus led up of the Spirit into the wilderness to be tempted of the devil.*

Again, Matthew records that Jesus was led:

How	Of the Spirit
Where	Into the Wilderness
Why	To be tempted of the devil

Sometimes, when we are going through our wilderness experiences, we will get flustered thinking that it is "the devil" and we rebuke and bind up and cast down, and tear up and trample on, and we neglect to go to God to just simply find out if this is his will concerning us. Some Christians see a demon in everything, and they glorify demonic activity, but I want us to change our thinking. Not everything is a demon. Some things are orchestrated by God, because we need to be stripped of our worldly inhibitions and thinking, we need to be purged, cleansed and sometimes we need strengthening and that will only come when we are close to God. When we draw close to God and pull away from the world, we will begin to see that some of the light afflictions, which are but for a moment are truly a present from God, as he aids us in getting rid of the weight and the sin which so easily besets us.

So Jesus went into the wilderness through the leading of the Spirit.

> Mat 4:2   And when he had fasted forty days and forty nights,
> he was afterward an hungred.

Notice verse 2 of Matthew chapter 4 records that Jesus had just finished fasting for forty days, immediately after this, the tempter came. What did he do, try to get him at a place where he was weak. He was hunger and so food would have been weighing heavily on his mind. The need to eat something must have been great. Please note: **Jesus had finished his fasting, so eating was not the issue.** The issue was the subject of the statement

a.   What do I mean? When a sentence is constructed, it is usually made up of what is known as

    i.   The Subject—i.e. something or someone: e.g. the little boy is riding the bike . . . here the little boy is the subject of

138

the sentence. What is happening is happening to the little boy, it is about him.

The Predicate - i.e. what that someone or something (the subject) is doing or what is being done to that someone or something (the subject)

So "riding the bike" is the predicate in the example sentence used above. Why am I pointing this out? Because sometimes we make an issue about the predicate and we miss the subject of the sentence. With this in mind, let us examine what the enemy said to Jesus in his first temptation, as recorded in verse 3

> *Mat 4:3*   *. . . he said "If thou be the Son of God, command that these stones be made bread".*

Subject: If thou (Jesus) be the son of God
Predicate: command that these stones be made bread

There was nothing wrong with him turning the stones into bread, he was more than able being God, however; that was not the issue. The issue was the subject; Satan started his statement by saying, "if thou be the son of God", let's not miss that. For Satan knew Jesus was the son of God, Satan knew Jesus was the flesh of God, which therefore means that Satan knew Jesus was divine. Satan questioned Jesus' identity. Not because he did not know who Jesus was, but rather tempting him to have his divine nature ruled by his flesh, his human nature. Tempting him by saying prove to me that you are the son of God, that you have divine power, that you are truly the flesh of God, for if you are, then you should be able to turn these stones into bread.

139

However, Jesus did not rise to the temptation, of; not just turning the stones into bread as hungry as he was, but rather; the temptation of letting his divine nature be ruled or directed by his human nature or fleshly desires, wants or needs, but rather he brought the Word:

> *Mat 4:4*   *But he answered and said, It is written, Man shall not live by bread alone, but by every word that proceedeth out of the mouth of God.*

Don't miss the reply: Jesus the human flesh of God said to the devil, his humanity shall not be sustained by bread alone, but rather by every ordained instruction from the Word of God, or rather his human nature will be led by his divine nature, not by his fleshly desires.

But the devil did not stop there, the scripture records that the devil then takes Jesus up into the holy city and set him on the highest area of the temple and there he tempted him even another time.

> Mat 4:5   Then the devil taketh him up into the holy city, and setteth him on a pinnacle of the temple,
> Mat 4:6   And saith unto him, If thou be the Son of God, cast thyself down: for it is written, He shall give his angels charge concerning thee: and in *their* hands they shall bear thee up, lest at any time thou dash thy foot against a stone.

Again, watch the subject: if thou be the son of God, (the predicate) cast thyself down, then the devil did something else, he also brought the word: for it is written He shall give his angels charge concerning thee: and in their hands they shall bear thee up, lest at any time thou dash thy foot against a stone.

Hold up now! Does the Bible say that? Yes, the Bible does say that, Satan knew the word. However, what I ask myself is this: Remember, every man is tempted when he is drawn away of his own lust and enticed. The bread was easy for Jesus was fasting for forty days, but why the holy city and why would casting himself down be enticing? The enemy knew he was talking to God. He knew that this was his creator, he knew that his word will not return unto him void, so what better way to tempt him than to use his words. It is such a dare: go on then, since you have charge over everything, throw yourself down and let's see if your angels will catch you? Let me see if those that did not follow me in rebellion still serve you?

How many times have you heard it said to us in church, remind God of his words (as though he has forgotten), he hasn't forgotten his words, rather he swears by them: He knows that his words must accomplish for he is the keeper of his words. How tempting must it have been for Jesus, but watch what he did: he once again did not rise to the challenge of proving anything to the devil. Rather he brought the word,

> Mat 4:7   Jesus said unto him, It is written again, Thou shalt
> not tempt the Lord thy God.

Jesus showed once again that his humanity was subjected to his divinity. He would not rise to the challenge of proving that his words would be kept, nor did he lose focus of his mission. His reason for coming to earth was not to prove that he is God, but rather to die for sinful man.

The devil wasn't satisfied, so once again, he tempted him. The Bible says

Mat 4:8	Again, the devil taketh him up into an exceeding high mountain, and sheweth him all the kingdoms of the world, and the glory of them;
Mat 4:9	And saith unto him, All these things will I give thee, if thou wilt fall down and worship me.

Questions: were the kingdoms of the world the devils' to give? And would that be tempting to Jesus? To both questions, the answer is yes. Yes it was the devils' to give. Why? Adam had lost dominion of the earthly kingdom giving it to the devil when he fell into sin. Satan had control of the worldly kingdom and yes if he gave it to Jesus there and then, then guess what? Jesus would not have to die for it; just give up his dominion to the devil. No blood would have had to be shed, but that meant the world would still be bound by sin. It also meant that Jesus would have committed idolatry, serving and worshipping Satan, and this would have caused him to completely fail on his mission, his reason for coming to earth would have had to be abandoned, for he would no longer have been the spotless lamb.

Now it can be reasoned, that Jesus being God, could not have committed sin! However, I beg to differ whilst agreeing, I present to you a bit of an oxymoron. It would not have been fair if Jesus wasn't all man and able to commit sin. Remember the scripture says, "he was tempted in all points like as we are, yet without sin"

> *Heb 4:15*   *For we have not an high priest which cannot be touched with the feeling of our infirmities; but was in all points tempted like as we are, yet without sin.*

He was very much a man. He lived on this earth and allowed himself to be subjected to everything that we as humans go through. He hungered, he tired, he slept, he had urges, and he was tempted, yet without sin. It would not have been fair for us, if Jesus was not actually tempted, nor would this scripture be true. For Hebrews 4:15 states, that Jesus can be touched with the feelings of our weaknesses, why? Because he went through what we went through, that is why he is our mediator. He is the best one to show mercy for he has gone through what we go through and allowed himself to be tempted. Now as God, he could not sin, for God cannot sin, but as man, he could have sinned. However, even greater yet, his humanity was always subject to his divinity, his fleshly nature was kept subject to his divine nature. That is why he made such statements like:

Joh 5:19	*...Verily, verily, I say unto you, The Son can do nothing of himself, but what he seeth the Father do: for what things soever he doeth, these also doeth the Son likewise.*
Joh 5:30	*I can of mine own self do nothing: as I hear, I judge: and my judgment is just; because I seek not mine own will, but the will of the Father which hath sent me.*
Joh 5:36	*But I have greater witness than that of John: for the works which the Father hath given me to finish, the same works that I do, bear witness of me, that the Father hath sent me.*

Jesus was in TOTAL submission: his human nature was subjected to his divine nature and of course his divine nature would not have led him into sin, therefore, he could not sin.

Oh I give God thanks; Jesus did not take the easy route out. Once again, he came again with the written word:

Mat 4:10   Then saith Jesus unto him, Get thee hence, Satan:

for it is written, Thou shalt worship the Lord thy
God, and him only shalt thou serve.

Jesus stayed in the written word: What kind of world would it be today, if Satan had gotten Jesus to break his own law. Remember, Jesus walked the earth during the dispensation of the Law: He had to keep the law and the commandments. One of which was "thou shalt not serve any other gods"

Exo 20:3   *Thou shalt have no other gods before me.*
Exo 20:5   *Thou shalt not bow down thyself to them, nor serve them: for I the LORD thy God am a jealous God, visiting the iniquity of the fathers upon the children unto the third and fourth generation of them that hate me;*

Jesus knew the word, and he also lived the word. He was the word made flesh, so no one can out quote Jesus, the word. This time Jesus put the word into action and rebuked the devil: telling him get thee hence. Jesus also once again showed his subjection, (paraphrasing) "this human nature shall worship only the Lord his God and him only will this nature serve". Only then did the devil leave him and when his temptation was over, angels came and ministered unto him.

Mat 4:11   Then the devil leaveth him, and, behold,
angels came and ministered unto him.

During his wilderness experience, Jesus endured great temptation. His identity was questioned, his flesh was weakened from being on a forty day fast, yet his Spirit was soaring and strong. He was strong in the word; he was set in his purpose and remained true to his mission.

Please note also, the scripture in St. Luke 4:14 declares

> Luk 4:14 And Jesus returned in the power of the Spirit into Galilee: and there went out a fame of him through all the region round about.

After Jesus' temptation and after his total submission, Jesus returned from the wilderness in the power of the Spirit. Jesus emerged from the wilderness in the power of the Spirit; however this power came only after victory in the wilderness.

Our Example

What better example can we take than that of Jesus Christ himself; he endured temptation at his weakest point. His victory came through his submission; his flesh was subject to his Spirit. Paul puts it eloquently when he said.

> 1Co 9:27 *But I keep under my body, and bring it into subjection: . . .*

In this lies our greatest strength, bringing our human nature into subjection to the divine will of God. For many times our flesh becomes our own enemy. The devil can tempt us all he wants, but he cannot make or force us to do anything, no matter how enticing. We however, can work ourselves into committing sin or yielding to that temptation. The book of first John chapter 3 verse 6 & 9 used to trouble me: for I could not understand why God would allow John to write:

1Jn 3:6	*Whosoever abideth in him sinneth not: whosoever sinneth hath not seen him, neither known him.*
1Jn 3:9	*Whosoever is born of God doth not commit sin; for his seed remaineth in him: and he cannot sin, because he is born of God.*

For I am born of God and considered myself to be abiding in God; yet I have sinned on many occasions. So for a long time that verse troubled me. I used to think John made an error and was just too heavenly minded and deep! However, after studying Jesus' wilderness experience, yes I will admit, it is doing this study that brought the revelation of that experience to my heart. (Pray for me . . . God is still working on me).

I now understand, the writer is not saying when you are baptised, nor when you get the Holy Ghost, nor when you are converted, but rather, when your human nature is in total submission to God's divine nature or God's will, you CANNOT sin. For if you are being led of God, God will never lead you into sin. James even helps us out to let us know it is not the devil that causes us to sin, he tempts us, but what is on the inside is what defiles us.

Jas 1:13	*Let no man say when he is tempted, I am tempted of God: for God cannot be tempted with evil, neither tempteth he any man:*
Jas 1:14	*But every man is tempted, when he is drawn away of his own lust, and enticed.*
Jas 1:15	*Then when lust hath conceived, it bringeth forth sin: and sin, when it is finished, bringeth forth death.*

Yes! I know we don't want to admit that we have some things (***our own lusts***) in us that causes us to be drawn away from God. It is our own desires, it is our own lusts, the devil will tempt us and even put us in compromising situations. However, we must have the will and the power to say no, to walk away, to rebuke the devil, to rise above our own lusts. We must be so submitted and subjected to the divine nature of God in us, the Holy Ghost; and draw from the word of God, using the necessary and vital scriptures to save our souls.

When we look further in Matthew beyond the temptation, we will see, after the wilderness experience, the victory Jesus had, then he began calling his disciples. The marriage in Cana, though not recorded in Matthew would have happened after this experience. John records that his disciples believed on him. Matthew records that it was after the wilderness experience that Jesus began calling his disciples and they were with him at the marriage in Cana.

Joh 2:1   And the third day there was a marriage in Cana of
            Galilee; and the mother of Jesus was there:
Joh 2:2   And both Jesus was called, and his disciples, to the
            marriage.

Therefore, he returned from the wilderness with all power and might of the Holy Ghost and in victory: then

1. Called his disciples
2. Then began his ministry

We often get it the wrong way round, for we want to be baptised, filled with the Holy Ghost, which is all good, but then we want to start our ministry and we haven't gone through or been victorious in our wildernesses.

We Must Be Trustworthy

Victory in our wilderness experience tells God that we are trust worthy. This salvation mission is too great for us to mess up. There are lives, families, communities, towns, cities, countries and nations at stake. God must know that he can trust us to allow him to lead us:

> *Exo 20:20*   *And Moses said unto the people, Fear not: for God is come to prove you, and that his fear may be before your faces, that ye sin not.*
>
> *Deu 8:2*   *And thou shalt remember all the way which the LORD thy God led thee these forty years in the wilderness, to humble thee, and to prove thee, to know what was in thine heart, whether thou wouldest keep his commandments, or no.*

God therefore will prove us, he will allow the devil to tempt us, for this will reveal more to us, than to God, what is really in our hearts. We don't know what we will do until we are faced with the situation. Many times we say we would never do a thing, and then when proven, or faced with that challenge, we end up doing the very thing we said we would not do.

> *Rom 7:19*   *For the good that I would I do not: but the evil which I would not, that I do.*

God needs us to know ourselves, he knows us and many times we make lofty promises to Him, which he knows we cannot keep. Therefore, God will allow the tempter to bring that situation upon us. God will allow us to go through a wilderness experience, and oops, lo and behold, we realise that we are not as submitted as we said. We often have good intentions, but what we do with those intentions is what sometimes count, especially in a matter of eternal life or eternal death.

Jesus' Ministry

Jesus even knew his timing; he began his ministry, picking up where his forerunner had left off in time and message.

Mat 4:12   Now when Jesus had heard that John was cast into prison, he departed into Galilee;

Mat 4:17   From that time Jesus began to preach, and to say, Repent: for the kingdom of heaven is at hand.

Fulfilling every prophecy, fulfilling every law, breaking none, Jesus proved that it is possible to live in this world and yet not be of the world. The ministry of Jesus Christ, though it lasted only three (3) and one third (1/3) years, had such great impact on the world because, as he explained, he and the Father are one. His human nature was so submitted to his divine nature, that the divine nature was the only nature from which he took instruction.

John 10:30   I and my Father are one

This wasn't just a verse just to prove Jesus is God, but also to show that the humanity had given full dominion and free course to the divinity and this is where our victory lies.

Jesus began calling his disciples and preaching in the synagogues.

Mat 4:18   And Jesus, walking by the sea of Galilee, saw two brethren, Simon called Peter, and Andrew his brother, casting a net into the sea: for they were fishers.

Mat 4:19   And he saith unto them, Follow me, and I will make you fishers of men.

| Mat 4:20 | And they straightway left *their* nets, and followed him. |
| Mat 4:21 | And going on from thence, he saw other two brethren, James *the son* of Zebedee, and John his brother, in a ship with Zebedee their father, mending their nets; and he called them. |

Every miracle Jesus set out to do was done, again not because he came as God, for he made it fair so that Hebrews 4:15 would be true. He walked the earth as man, showing us that we can have dominion over sin, showing us that we do have the power to defeat Satan even at his best game. Our victory lies in total consecration and submission to God.

Mat 4:22	And they immediately left the ship and their father, and followed him.
Mat 4:23	And Jesus went about all Galilee, teaching in their synagogues, and preaching the gospel of the kingdom, and healing all manner of sickness and all manner of disease among the people.
Mat 4:24	And his fame went throughout all Syria: and they brought unto him all sick people that were taken with divers diseases and torments, and those which were possessed with devils, and those which were lunatick, and those that had the palsy; and he healed them.

Jesus's Mission Fulfilled

Salvation is now a reality! For the lamb slain from the foundation of the world, before time, has been manifested in time, at Calvary, and those who receive him and believe on him can partake of the life he gives. His mission was to die so that we might live. He was crucified and his blood was shed as the prophets foretold. This blood which has the power to redeem all of mankind is still flowing today. No message has greater impact, no blood loss has greater effect, no story has been told more. For what Jesus set out to do, has been done.

But it didn't end at Calvary. He has left us the great commission to lead men to this great salvation, through teaching and baptism. Now, because he has given us this mission, he must ensure that we too do not fail. Hence the need for us to be proven: Our wilderness experiences are necessary for the saving of souls. For when we have endured, and come through victoriously, then our ministry will have a greater impact. Our message will not just be of what we have heard, seen or read, but rather of what we have lived. It is great to tell the testimony of Moses, but greater still are our own testimonies of wildernesses that we have endured and come through with God, victoriously. We will be more convinced about God, we will be doubly sure that God is more than able.

You cannot convince me of something you are not yourself convinced about. You cannot cause me to be passionate about something you are not passionate about. You cannot get me excited about something you are not excited about. You will either have experienced it yourself and be able to convince me of what you have experienced, or it will be clear that you have not experienced what you speak of, and therefore unable to convince me.

I share another story I have heard about the eagle: Dr. Mark Hanby shared a story about something he experienced as a child. He was taken for the first time to the zoo and in his excitement running to see all the animals he was distracted by something happening by the aviary. He approached and through the crowds he saw some eagles. They were all sitting on the branches just minding their own business, looking comfortable, except for one. One particular bird was flapping his large wings about and flying into the fence as though he was testing each area for a weak point, somewhere he could escape. He would make very loud sounds and flap around obviously trying to get out. The eagle would work himself up, rest and then be at it again. Dr. Hanby said, the Aviary keeper then said, it is not hard to tell which ones were born in captivity, is it?

Most of the eagles there were born in captivity they were hatched in the cages and spent all their lives living like ordinary birds, on the low lands, eating what they were fed and not being bothered about it, Why? Because they did not know any different, they were born and had always been in captivity. They did not know that they could soar on the wings at heights so far that no other bird can reach. They were not aware that they have the ability to hunt clutching their mighty claws over other animals rendering them defenceless, they would not convince anyone that they were eagles (if you could not see them). But this one eagle, he wasn't born in captivity, he knew what it was to soar at very high altitudes, he knew what it felt like to hunt, he knew he was designed for flight, he had felt the wind under his wings and knew he was not supposed to be on the ground he was not made for the lowlands and so he could not be comfortable just living like a chicken. He needed to get back to what he was used to. He had the experience of flight, and this eagle wanted to do what he knew.

So is it with us, we must do what we are called to do, but we will only ever know our true potential when we are submitted to God. We must have the fire of God in our souls pushing us on to new heights. New heights in God does not come through fighting with each other, it doesn't come from tearing down or stepping on each other, rather it comes through going low, so low that you are not seen, becoming hidden in Christ. We must humble ourselves under the mighty hand of God and he will exalt us in due time.

> *1Pe 5:6   Humble yourselves therefore under the mighty hand of God, that he may exalt you in due time:*

God is not mocked, he is the keeper of his word, and he knows our hearts. We must allow the hand of God to work in our lives. I will be the first to say it is not always easy nor is it pain free. I will also declare and confess, that I too am following on to know, I am not one who has all the answers, (God does); but I do know there are times when we struggle with our trials, we struggle with our challenges, we mess up and we falter, we try to "fix" things ourselves. Whether through our lack of faith, lack of trust or a life that is not fully submitted, we only do ourselves and others a grave injustice when we fail to let go and let God.

Questions for Chapter 10:

1. In no less than 1500 words, choose three other items of the tabernacle, and give their significance to Jesus Christ.
2. In your own words, exhort on how to be fully and completely submitted to God.

Conclusion

Through his submission, Jesus' ministry soared to new heights, his miracles were innumerable, his impact was far reaching; stretching all the way through the chronicles of time, the corridors of the past gave way to his salvation message as he ventured into hell and freed souls which were being held captive.

> *Eph 4:9*   *(Now that he ascended, what is it but that he also descended first into the lower parts of the earth?*
>
> *1Pe 3:19*   *By which also he went and preached unto the spirits in prison;*
>
> *1Pe 3:20*   *Which sometime were disobedient, when once the longsuffering of God waited in the days of Noah, while the ark was a preparing, wherein few, that is, eight souls were saved by water.*

It stretched through the corridors of the future to save us who were not present when he walked the earth, yet we are still recipients of his grace, his love, his mercy, his kindness, and even more so, his salvation. What impact, all because he was submitted to the Father, the humanity of Christ was totally submitted to the divinity of Christ.

Our wilderness experiences are not just for us, but rather for those who will be impacted by our testimonies, after we have overcome.

Summary

Moses' impact as the leader or deliverer was great, today it is impossible to teach on leadership without touching on Moses. This is due to the fact that after struggling a while with what he was to do, Moses finally submitted himself to God. Remember how long his conversation with God was and the many excuses he gave when God sent him back to Egypt? However, when he finally submitted himself to what he was ordained to do, look at the impact he had. He is still considered the greatest leader who ever lived.

David struggled with his lost. He lost a lot when he was forced to run because he was being chased by Saul, all because he was anointed. He also struggled with his calling, being anointed to be king. However; he did not expect the route God took, it caught him off guard for a while. Hence he ended up in the Philistines camp and was ready to go against what he was called to do. But God! God is faithful to his promise over our lives. God stepped in and stopped David from killing off the very sheep he was called to shepherd over. When he finally submitted himself, he was and is still hailed today as Israel's greatest king. What an impact when we submit ourselves to God. David's influence with his men was so great that they were willing to die for him, to get him anything he wanted.

Job's endurance and victory in his wilderness gave him greater wealth than he had prior to going through. The Bible records that God turned the captivity of Job, when he prayed for his friends; the Bible records that it was after praying for his friends that Job was blessed with twice as much as he had before.

Job 42:10	And the LORD turned the captivity of Job, when he prayed for his friends: also the LORD gave Job twice as much as he had before.
Job 42:12	So the LORD blessed the latter end of Job more than his beginning: for he had fourteen thousand sheep, and six thousand camels, and a thousand yoke of oxen, and a thousand she asses.

Can I just paused right now and say: this is probably the hardest part of our wilderness experiences. When we see others as being part of the reason we are going through, it is going to be that much harder to move pass the hurt and get to our blessing. For that process requires us to pray for those who persecuted us and despitefully used us. As long as we see them as the object of our wilderness we will struggle. Be reminded, Jesus was led in the wilderness by the Spirit. They may be the ones God used to propel us through our wilderness in order to get us to our ministry, but please don't miss it, it's all God's doing and if we submit ourselves to his work, it will be marvellous in our eyes.

Let us not lose focus, regardless of what people may do or say, remember, God is taking us through the wilderness to move us to another dimension, it is a transitional vehicle. For the mission you have is too great for you to fail.

Job's blessing was double for his trouble, and his daughters were fairer than all the women in the land.

Job 42:15	And in all the land were no women found *so* fair as the daughters of Job: and their father gave them inheritance among their brethren.

It would be so easy for us to endure affliction when we can see or we know the prize. That knowledge spurs us on and propels us to give our all in succeeding. We know the ultimate prize is heaven, we will receive eternal life at the end of this journey, but how often does that seem to not be enough when we are faced with struggles. If the canopy of heaven were transparent and we could see heaven with our naked eyes, then I think many of us would try harder to please God. Unfortunately, that is not God's way, he requires us to trust him, he requires us to believe his word, he requires our faith, unwavering. This means then that he will not be dangling heaven for you to see. You must believe that God is and that he is a rewarder of them that are diligent in seeking him.

> *Heb 11:6*   *But without faith it is impossible to please him: for he that cometh to God must believe that he is, and that he is a rewarder of them that diligently seek him.*

Job's faith was unmatched, even at his worst, he held on to his faith and to his integrity.

Sadly though, not all the wilderness experiences were victorious ones. For the children of Israel had so much, yet gained so little. They had Moses, the greatest leader, they had the prophecy of the deliverer, they had witnessed the miracles of God, showing mercy upon Israel, whilst bringing judgment upon Egypt. They had miracles such as: water from a rock, on more than one occasion, angels food to eat, quail enough to feed millions, a pillar of fire by night, a cloud by day that led them; they could see the visible manifestation of God, they had the greatest shadow of the plan of salvation, yet with only an eleven day journey, they failed and ended up losing out on their promise, whilst being cursed to wander in the wilderness for forty years.

158

Let me point out that it was never God's plan to slay them in the wilderness, but they never did submit themselves to God. Even with the miracles they experienced, they all died (except for Joshua and Caleb), as one by one their carcasses fell in the wilderness. Their little ones, who did not experience the miracles done in Egypt were the ones who entered the Promised Land. A people who did not know their God; these were born in the wilderness and had only heard of the many miracles, but had not seen them with their own eyes.

Be assured then, that the will of God must be done, and it is his will for you to accomplish what he has set out for you to do. However, also know that he is able to raise up stones. God's will must be done, and no one can hold him at ransom. God does not need us, but he chooses to use us in his plan. I am not saying that if someone else is used to do what you were intended to do, that it will be done as you would have done it, maybe not, for God has chosen you to do what you do best. However; his word must be accomplished, whether it is through one or the other, God's word will not return unto him void.

> *Isa 55:11*   *So shall my word be that goeth forth out of my mouth:*
>
> *it shall not return unto me void, but it shall accomplish that which I please, and it shall prosper in the thing whereto I sent it.*

As we see from the example of the Children of Israel, the Promised Land was occupied by Israelites. They went in, but not how God had intended, and not when he intended either.

✠ *Jas 4:7*   *Submit yourselves therefore to God. Resist the devil, and he will flee from you.*

This is one of the most misquoted scriptures of the Bible: For most will say, ". . . resist the devil and he will flee" yet we miss the greatest meaning and power of the verse . . . which is "submit yourselves therefore to God". Jesus showed this in his wilderness experience, his temptations came, but his answers showed the enemy that his flesh was under subjection to the Spirit.

Because of this secret, Jesus could resist rising to the temptation of proving his identity, as the "Son of God". Jesus knew he was the son of God, the devil also knew he was the son of God, but Jesus proved that above showing off his power he would show off his submission. His submission yielded much greater rewards.

In closing, above all else, be submitted to God, for when we are submitted to God, we will accomplish so much more, why? For the people who know their God, those who have a relationship with him, who've been through the wilderness, drawing close to him and have embraced their purpose, submitting their fleshly nature to God and adorning their spirits with his will, they shall do exploits.

Dan 11:32   *And such as do wickedly against the covenant shall he corrupt by flatteries: but the people that do know their God shall be strong, and do exploits.*

Be blessed and endure your wilderness experiences in Jesus Name!

2Ti 2:3   *Thou therefore endure hardness, as a good soldier of Jesus Christ.*

Appendices

These appendices contain an extensive reference regarding the occurrences of wilderness in the scriptures. Within these pages, you'll find meanings to the number of occurrences; in each book and each segment (Old Testament and New Testament). Much of this reference has to be attributed to James Strong, LL.D., S.T.D. as it is extracted from The New Strong's Exhaustive Concordance of the Bible; where much of the work had already been done and included.

Appendix A

Wilderness Occurrences (Bible Books)

Old Testament Books (which mentions the word wilderness)

Genesis: 7 times	Exodus: 23 times	Leviticus: 4 times
Numbers: 45 times	Deuteronomy: 19 times	Joshua: 15 times
Judges: 9 times	1 Samuel: 18 times	2 Samuel: 6 times
1 Kings: 4 times	2 Kings: 1 once	1 Chronicles: 4
2 Chronicles: 6 times	Nehemiah: twice	Job: 6 times
Psalms: 23 times	Proverbs: once	Songs of Solomon: twice
Isaiah: 20 times	Jeremiah: 21 times	Lamentations: 3 times
Ezekiel:15 times	Hosea: 5 times	Joel: 5 times
Amos: 3 times	Zephaniah: once, and	Malachi: once

New Testament Books (which mentions the word wilderness)

Matthew: 5 times, Mark: 5 times, Luke: 7 times, John:3 times, Acts:7 times, 1 Corinthians: once, 2 Corinthians: once, Hebrews: twice and Revelations:3 Times.

Appendix B
Total Number of Occurrences

The total occurrences of "wilderness" in the scriptures are broken down as follows:

- Old Testament: 271 Occurrences
- New Testament: 34 occurrences
- Entire Bible: 305 occurrences

Appendix C

All Scriptures Pertaining to Wilderness (KJV)

30

[30]Scripture Verse	Strong's #	Scripture
Genesis 14:6	4057	And the Horites in their mount Seir, unto Elparan, which is by the wilderness.
Genesis 16:7	4057	And the angel of the LORD found her by a fountain of water in the wilderness, by the fountain in the way to Shur.
Genesis 21:14	4057	And Abraham rose up early in the morning, and took bread, and a bottle of water, and gave it unto Hagar, putting it on her shoulder, and the child, and sent her away: and she departed, and wandered in the wilderness of Beersheba.
Genesis 21:20-21	4057	And God was with the lad; and he grew, and dwelt in the wilderness, and became an archer. And he dwelt in the wilderness of Paran: and his mother took him a wife out of the land of Egypt.
Genesis 36:24	4057	And these are the children of Zibeon; both Ajah, and Anah: this was that Anah that found the mules in the wilderness, as he fed the asses of
Genesis 37:22	4057	And Reuben said unto them, Shed no blood, but cast him into this pit that is in the wilderness, and lay no hand upon him; that he might rid him out of their hands, to deliver him to his father again.
Exodus 3:18	4057	And they shall hearken to thy voice: and thou shalt come, thou and the elders of Israel, unto the king of Egypt, and ye shall say unto him, The LORD God of the Hebrews hath met with us: and now let us go, we beseech thee, three days' journey into the wilderness, that we may sacrifice to the LORD our God.
Exodus 4:27	4057	And the LORD said to Aaron, Go into the wilderness to meet Moses. And he went, and met him in the mount of God, and kissed him.

---

[30] **All Scripture Verses used**—King James Version of the Bible (Unless otherwise stated)

Exodus 5:1	4057	And afterward Moses and Aaron went in, and told Pharaoh, Thus saith the LORD God of Israel, Let my people go, that they may hold a feast unto me in the wilderness.
Exodus 7:16	4057	And thou shalt say unto him, The LORD God of the Hebrews hath sent me unto thee, saying, Let my people go, that they may serve me in the wilderness: and, behold, hitherto thou wouldest not hear.
Exodus 8:27-28	4057	We will go three days' journey into the wilderness, and sacrifice to the LORD our God, as he shall command us. And Pharaoh said, I will let you go, that ye may sacrifice to the LORD your God in the wilderness; only ye shall not go very far away: intreat for me.
Exodus 13:18	4057	But God led the people about, through the way of the wilderness of the Red sea: and the children of Israel went up harnessed out of the land of Egypt.
Exodus 13:20	4057	And they took their journey from Succoth, and encamped in Etham, in the edge of the wilderness.
Exodus 14:3	4057	For Pharaoh will say of the children of Israel, They are entangled in the land, the wilderness hath shut them in.
Exodus 14:11-12	4057	And they said unto Moses, Because there were no graves in Egypt, hast thou taken us away to die in the wilderness? wherefore hast thou dealt thus with us, to carry us forth out of Egypt? Is not this the word that we did tell thee in Egypt, saying, Let us alone, that we may serve the Egyptians? For it had been better for us to serve the Egyptians, than that we should die in the wilderness.
Exodus 15:22	4057	So Moses brought Israel from the Red sea, and they went out into the wilderness of Shur; and they went three days in the wilderness, and found no water.

Exodus 16:1-3	4057	And they took their journey from Elim, and all the congregation of the children of Israel came unto the wilderness of Sin, which is between Elim and Sinai, on the fifteenth day of the second month after their departing out of the land of Egypt. And the whole congregation of the children of Israel murmured against Moses and Aaron in the wilderness: And the children of Israel said unto them, Would to God we had died by the hand of the LORD in the land of Egypt, when we sat by the flesh pots, and when we did eat bread to the full; for ye have brought us forth into this wilderness, to kill this whole assembly with hunger
Exodus 16:10	4057	And it came to pass, as Aaron spake unto the whole congregation of the children of Israel, that they looked toward the wilderness, and, behold, the glory of the LORD appeared in the cloud.
Exodus 16:14	4057	And when the dew that lay was gone up, behold, upon the face of the wilderness there lay a small round thing, as small as the hoar frost on the ground.
Exodus 16:32	4057	And Moses said, This is the thing which the LORD commandeth, Fill an omer of it to be kept for your generations; that they may see the bread wherewith I have fed you in the wilderness, when I brought you forth from the land of Egypt.
Exodus 17:1	4057	And all the congregation of the children of Israel journeyed from the wilderness of Sin, after their journeys, according to the commandment of the LORD, and pitched in Rephidim: and there was no water for the people to drink.
Exodus 18:5	4057	And Jethro, Moses' father in law, came with his sons and his wife unto Moses into the wilderness, where he encamped at the mount of God:
Exodus 19:1-2	4057	In the third month, when the children of Israel were gone forth out of the land of Egypt, the same day came they into the wilderness of Sinai. For they were departed from Rephidim, and were come to the desert of Sinai, and had pitched in the wilderness; and there Israel camped before the mount.

Leviticus 7:38	4057	Which the LORD commanded Moses in mount Sinai, in the day that he commanded the children of Israel to offer their oblations unto the LORD, in the wilderness of Sinai.
Leviticus 16:10	4057	But the goat, on which the lot fell to be the scapegoat, shall be presented alive before the LORD, to make an atonement with him, and to let him go for a scapegoat into the
Leviticus 16:21-22	4057	And Aaron shall lay both his hands upon the head of the live goat, and confess over him all the iniquities of the children of Israel, and all their transgressions in all their sins, putting them upon the head of the goat, and shall send him away by the hand of a fit man into the wilderness: And the goat shall bear upon him all their iniquities unto a land not inhabited: and he shall let go the goat in the wilderness.
Numbers 1:1	4057	And the LORD spake unto Moses in the wilderness of Sinai, in the tabernacle of the congregation, on the first day of the second month, in the second year after they were come out of the land of Egypt, saying,
Numbers 1:19	4057	As the LORD commanded Moses, so he numbered them in the wilderness of Sinai.
Numbers 3:4	4057	And Nadab and Abihu died before the LORD, when they offered strange fire before the LORD, in the wilderness of Sinai, and they had no children: and Eleazar and Ithamar ministered in the priest's office in the sight of Aaron their father.
Numbers 3:14	4057	And the LORD spake unto Moses in the wilderness of Sinai, saying,
Numbers 9:1	4057	And the LORD spake unto Moses in the wilderness of Sinai, in the first month of the second year after they were come out of the land of Egypt, saying,
Numbers 9:5	4057	And they kept the passover on the fourteenth day of the first month at even in the wilderness of Sinai: according to all that the LORD commanded Moses, so did the children of Israel.

Numbers 10:12	4057	And the children of Israel took their journeys out of the wilderness of Sinai; and the cloud rested in the wilderness of Paran.
Numbers 10:31	4057	And he said, Leave us not, I pray thee; forasmuch as thou knowest how we are to encamp in the wilderness, and thou mayest be to us instead of eyes
Numbers 12:16	4057	And afterward the people removed from Hazeroth, and pitched in the wilderness of Paran.
Numbers 13:3	4057	And Moses by the commandment of the LORD sent them from the wilderness of Paran: all those men were heads of the children of Israel
Numbers 13:21	4057	So they went up, and searched the land from the wilderness of Zin unto Rehob, as men come to Hamath.
Numbers 13:26	4057	And they went and came to Moses, and to Aaron, and to all the congregation of the children of Israel, unto the wilderness of Paran, to Kadesh; and brought back word unto them, and unto all the congregation, and shewed them the fruit of the land.
Numbers 14:2	4057	And all the children of Israel murmured against Moses and against Aaron: and the whole congregation said unto them, Would God that we had died in the land of Egypt! or would God we had died in this wilderness!
Numbers 14:16	4057	Because the LORD was not able to bring this people into the land which he sware unto them, therefore he hath slain them in the wilderness.
Numbers 14:22	4057	Because all those men which have seen my glory, and my miracles, which I did in Egypt and in the wilderness, and have tempted me now these ten times, and have not hearkened to my voice;
Numbers 14:25	4057	(Now the Amalekites and the Canaanites dwelt in the valley.) To morrow turn you, and get you into the wilderness by the way of the Red sea.
Numbers 14:29	4057	Your carcases shall fall in this wilderness; and all that were numbered of you, according to your whole number, from twenty years old and upward, which have murmured against me,

Numbers 14:32-33	4057	But as for you, your carcases, they shall fall in this wilderness. And your children shall wander in the wilderness forty years, and bear your whoredoms, until your carcases be wasted in the wilderness.
Numbers 14:35	4057	I the LORD have said, I will surely do it unto all this evil congregation, that are gathered together against me: in this wilderness they shall be consumed, and there they shall die.
Numbers 15:32	4057	And while the children of Israel were in the wilderness, they found a man that gathered sticks upon the sabbath day.
Numbers 16:13	4057	Is it a small thing that thou hast brought us up out of a land that floweth with milk and honey, to kill us in the wilderness, except thou make thyself altogether a prince over us?
Numbers 20:4	4057	And why have ye brought up the congregation of the LORD into this wilderness, that we and our cattle should die there?
Numbers 21:5	4057	And the people spake against God, and against Moses, Wherefore have ye brought us up out of Egypt to die in the wilderness? for there is no bread, neither is there any water; and our soul loatheth this light bread.
Numbers 21:11	4057	And they journeyed from Oboth, and pitched at Ijeabarim, in the wilderness which is before Moab, toward the sunrising
Numbers 21:13	4057	From thence they removed, and pitched on the other side of Arnon, which is in the wilderness that cometh out of the coasts of the Amorites: for Arnon is the border of Moab, between Moab and the Amorites
Numbers 21:18	4057	The princes digged the well, the nobles of the people digged it, by the direction of the lawgiver, with their staves. And from the wilderness they went to Mattanah:
Numbers 21:23	4057	And Sihon would not suffer Israel to pass through his border: but Sihon gathered all his people together, and went out against Israel into the wilderness: and he came to Jahaz, and fought

Numbers 24:1	4057	And when Balaam saw that it pleased the LORD to bless Israel, he went not, as at other times, to seek for enchantments, but he set his face toward the wilderness
Numbers 26:64-65	4057	But among these there was not a man of them whom Moses and Aaron the priest numbered, when they numbered the children of Israel in the wilderness of Sinai. For the LORD had said of them, They shall surely die in the wilderness. And there was not left a man of them, save Caleb the son of Jephunneh, and Joshua the son of Nun.
Numbers 27:3	4057	Our father died in the wilderness, and he was not in the company of them that gathered themselves together against the LORD in the company of Korah; but died in his own sin, and had no sons.
Numbers 27:14	4057	For ye rebelled against my commandment in the desert of Zin, in the strife of the congregation, to sanctify me at the water before their eyes: that is the water of Meribah in Kadesh in the wilderness of Zin.
Numbers 32:13	4057	And the LORD'S anger was kindled against Israel, and he made them wander in the wilderness forty years, until all the generation, that had done evil in the sight of the LORD, was consumed.
Numbers 32:15	4057	For if ye turn away from after him, he will yet again leave them in the wilderness; and ye shall destroy all this people.
Numbers 33:6	4057	And they departed from Succoth, and pitched in Etham, which is in the edge of the wilderness.
Numbers 33:8	4057	And they departed from before Pihahiroth, and passed through the midst of the sea into the wilderness, and went three days' journey in the wilderness of Etham, and pitched in Marah
Numbers 33:11-12	4057	And they removed from the Red sea, and encamped in the wilderness of Sin. And they took their journey out of the wilderness of Sin, and encamped in Dophkah
Numbers 33:15	4057	And they departed from Rephidim, and pitched in the wilderness of Sinai.

Numbers 33:36	4057	Then your south quarter shall be from the wilderness of Zin along by the coast of Edom, and your south border shall be the outmost coast of the salt sea eastward:
Deuteronomy 1:1	4057	These be the words which Moses spake unto all Israel on this side Jordan in the wilderness, in the plain over against the Red sea, between Paran, and Tophel, and Laban, and Hazeroth, and Dizahab.
Deuteronomy 1:19	4057	And when we departed from Horeb, we went through all that great and terrible wilderness, which ye saw by the way of the mountain of the Amorites, as the LORD our God commanded us; and we came to Kadeshbarnea
Deuteronomy 1:31	4057	And in the wilderness, where thou hast seen how that the LORD thy God bare thee, as a man doth bear his son, in all the way that ye went, until ye came into this place
Deuteronomy 1:40	4057	But as for you, turn you, and take your journey into the wilderness by the way of the Red sea.
Deuteronomy 2:1	4057	Then we turned, and took our journey into the wilderness by the way of the Red sea, as the LORD spake unto me: and we compassed mount Seir many days
Deuteronomy 2:7-8	4057	For the LORD thy God hath blessed thee in all the works of thy hand: he knoweth thy walking through this great wilderness: these forty years the LORD thy God hath been with thee; thou hast lacked nothing. And when we passed by from our brethren the children of Esau, which dwelt in Seir, through the way of the plain from Elath, and from Eziongaber, we turned and passed by the way of the wilderness of Moab.
Deuteronomy 2:26	4057	And I sent messengers out of the wilderness of Kedemoth unto Sihon king of Heshbon with words of peace, saying,
Deuteronomy 4:43	4057	Namely, Bezer in the wilderness, in the plain country, of the Reubenites; and Ramoth in Gilead, of the Gadites; and Golan in Bashan, of the Manassites.

Deuteronomy 8:2	4057	And thou shalt remember all the way which the LORD thy God led thee these forty years in the wilderness, to humble thee, and to prove thee, to know what was in thine heart, whether thou wouldest keep his commandments, or no.
Deuteronomy 8:15-16	4057	Who led thee through that great and terrible wilderness, wherein were fiery serpents, and scorpions, and drought, where there was no water; who brought thee forth water out of the rock of flint; Who fed thee in the wilderness with manna, which thy fathers knew not, that he might humble thee, and that he might prove thee, to do thee good at thy latter end;
Deuteronomy 9:7	4057	Remember, and forget not, how thou provokedst the LORD thy God to wrath in the wilderness: from the day that thou didst depart out of the land of Egypt, until ye came unto this place, ye have been rebellious against the LORD.
Deuteronomy 9:28	4057	Lest the land whence thou broughtest us out say, Because the LORD was not able to bring them into the land which he promised them, and because he hated them, he hath brought them out to slay them in the wilderness.
Deuteronomy 11:5	4057	And what he did unto you in the wilderness, until ye came into this place;
Deuteronomy 11:24	4057	Every place whereon the soles of your feet shall tread shall be yours: from the wilderness and Lebanon, from the river, the river Euphrates, even unto the uttermost sea shall your coast be.
Deuteronomy 29:5	4057	And I have led you forty years in the wilderness: your clothes are not waxen old upon you, and thy shoe is not waxen old upon thy foot.
Deuteronomy 32:10	3452	He found him in a desert land, and in the waste howling wilderness; he led him about, he instructed him, he kept him as the apple of his eye.
Deuteronomy 32:51	4057	Because ye trespassed against me among the children of Israel at the waters of Meribah-Kadesh, in the wilderness of Zin; because ye sanctified me not in the midst of the children of Israel

Joshua 1:4	4057	From the wilderness and this Lebanon even unto the great river, the river Euphrates, all the land of the Hittites, and unto the great sea toward the going down of the sun, shall be your coast
Joshua 5:4-6	4057	And this is the cause why Joshua did circumcise: All the people that came out of Egypt, that were males, even all the men of war, died in the wilderness by the way, after they came out of Egypt. Now all the people that came out were circumcised: but all the people that were born in the wilderness by the way as they came forth out of Egypt, them they had not circumcised. For the children of Israel walked forty years in the wilderness, till all the people that were men of war, which came out of Egypt, were consumed, because they obeyed not the voice of the LORD: unto whom the LORD sware that he would not shew them the land, which the LORD sware unto their fathers that he would give us, a land that floweth with milk and honey.
Joshua 8:15	4057	And Joshua and all Israel made as if they were beaten before them, and fled by the way of the wilderness.
Joshua 8:20	4057	And when the men of Ai looked behind them, they saw, and, behold, the smoke of the city ascended up to heaven, and they had no power to flee this way or that way: and the people that fled to the wilderness turned back upon the pursuers.
Joshua 12:8	4057	In the mountains, and in the valleys, and in the plains, and in the springs, and in the wilderness, and in the south country; the Hittites, the Amorites, and the Canaanites, the Perizzites, the Hivites, and the Jebusites:
Joshua 14:10	4057	And now, behold, the LORD hath kept me alive, as he said, these forty and five years, even since the LORD spake this word unto Moses, while the children of Israel wandered in the wilderness: and now, lo, I am this day fourscore and five years old.

Joshua 15:1	4057	This then was the lot of the tribe of the children of Judah by their families; even to the border of Edom the wilderness of Zin southward was the uttermost part of the south coast.
Joshua 15:61	4057	In the wilderness, Betharabah, Middin, and Secacah
Joshua 16:1	4057	And the lot of the children of Joseph fell from Jordan by Jericho, unto the water of Jericho on the east, to the wilderness that goeth up from Jericho throughout mount Bethel,
Joshua 18:12	4057	And their border on the north side was from Jordan; and the border went up to the side of Jericho on the north side, and went up through the mountains westward; and the goings out thereof were at the wilderness of Bethaven
Joshua 20:8	4057	And on the other side Jordan by Jericho eastward, they assigned Bezer in the wilderness upon the plain out of the tribe of Reuben, and Ramoth in Gilead out of the tribe of Gad, and Golan in Bashan out of the tribe of Manasseh.
Joshua 24:7	4057	And when they cried unto the LORD, he put darkness between you and the Egyptians, and brought the sea upon them, and covered them; and your eyes have seen what I have done in Egypt: and ye dwelt in the wilderness a long season.
Judges 1:16	4057	And the children of the Kenite, Moses' father in law, went up out of the city of palm trees with the children of Judah into the wilderness of Judah, which lieth in the south of Arad; and they went and dwelt among the people.
Judges 8:7	4057	And Gideon said, Therefore when the LORD hath delivered Zebah and Zalmunna into mine hand, then I will tear your flesh with the thorns of the wilderness and with briers
Judges 8:16	4057	And he took the elders of the city, and thorns of the wilderness and briers, and with them he taught the men of Succoth
Judges 11:16	4057	But when Israel came up from Egypt, and walked through the wilderness unto the Red sea, and came to Kadesh;

Judges 11:18	4057	Then they went along through the wilderness, and compassed the land of Edom, and the land of Moab, and came by the east side of the land of Moab, and pitched on the other side of Arnon, but came not within the border of Moab: for Arnon was the border of Moab
Judges 11:22	4057	And they possessed all the coasts of the Amorites, from Arnon even unto Jabbok, and from the wilderness even unto Jordan.
Judges 20:42	4057	Therefore they turned their backs before the men of Israel unto the way of the wilderness; but the battle overtook them; and them which came out of the cities they destroyed in the midst of them.
Judges 20:45	4057	And they turned and fled toward the wilderness unto the rock of Rimmon: and they gleaned of them in the highways five thousand men; and pursued hard after them unto Gidom, and slew two thousand men of them
Judges 20:47	4057	But six hundred men turned and fled to the wilderness unto the rock Rimmon, and abode in the rock Rimmon four months.
1 Samuel 4:8	4057	Woe unto us! who shall deliver us out of the hand of these mighty Gods? these are the Gods that smote the Egyptians with all the plagues in the wilderness.
1 Samuel 13:18	4057	And another company turned the way to Bethhoron: and another company turned to the way of the border that looketh to the valley of Zeboim toward the wilderness.
1 Samuel 17:28	4057	And Eliab his eldest brother heard when he spake unto the men; and Eliab's anger was kindled against David, and he said, Why camest thou down hither? and with whom hast thou left those few sheep in the wilderness? I know thy pride, and the naughtiness of thine heart; for thou art come down that thou mightest see the battle

1 Samuel 23:14-15	4057	And David abode in the wilderness in strong holds, and remained in a mountain in the wilderness of Ziph. And Saul sought him every day, but God delivered him not into his hand. And David saw that Saul was come out to seek his life: and David was in the wilderness of Ziph in a wood.
1 Samuel 23:24-25	4057	And they arose, and went to Ziph before Saul: but David and his men were in the wilderness of Maon, in the plain on the south of Jeshimon. Saul also and his men went to seek him. And they told David: wherefore he came down into a rock, and abode in the wilderness of Maon. And when Saul heard that, he pursued after David in the wilderness of Maon.
1 Samuel 24:1	4057	And it came to pass, when Saul was returned from following the Philistines, that it was told him, saying, Behold, David is in the wilderness of Engedi
1 Samuel 25:1	4057	And Samuel died; and all the Israelites were gathered together, and lamented him, and buried him in his house at Ramah. And David arose,
1 Samuel 25:4	4057	And David heard in the wilderness that Nabal did shear his sheep.
1 Samuel 25:14	4057	But one of the young men told Abigail, Nabal's wife, saying, Behold, David sent messengers out of the wilderness to salute our master; and he railed on them
1 Samuel 25:21	4057	Now David had said, Surely in vain have I kept all that this fellow hath in the wilderness, so that nothing was missed of all that pertained unto him: and he hath requited me evil for good.
1 Samuel 26:2-3	4057	Then Saul arose, and went down to the wilderness of Ziph, having three thousand chosen men of Israel with him, to seek David in the wilderness of Ziph. And Saul pitched in the hill of Hachilah, which is before Jeshimon, by the way. But David abode in the wilderness, and he saw that Saul came after him into the wilderness

2 Samuel 2:24	4057	Joab also and Abishai pursued after Abner: and the sun went down when they were come to the hill of Ammah, that lieth before Giah by the way of the wilderness of Gibeon.
2 Samuel 15:23	4057	And all the country wept with a loud voice, and all the people passed over: the king also himself passed over the brook Kidron, and all the people passed over, toward the way of the wilderness.
2 Samuel 15:28	4057	See, I will tarry in the plain of the wilderness, until there come word from you to certify me.
2 Samuel 16:2	4057	And the king said unto Ziba, What meanest thou by these? And Ziba said, The asses be for the king's household to ride on; and the bread and summer fruit for the young men to eat; and the wine, that such as be faint in the wilderness may drink.
2 Samuel 17:16	4057	Now therefore send quickly, and tell David, saying, Lodge not this night in the plains of the wilderness, but speedily pass over; lest the king be swallowed up, and all the people that are with him.
2 Samuel 17:29	4057	And honey, and butter, and sheep, and cheese of kine, for David, and for the people that were with him, to eat: for they said, The people is hungry, and weary, and thirsty, in the wilderness.
1 Kings 2:34	4057	So Benaiah the son of Jehoiada went up, and fell upon him, and slew him: and he was buried in his own house in the wilderness.
1 Kings 9:18	4057	And Baalath, and Tadmor in the wilderness, in the land,
1 Kings 19:4	4057	But he himself went a day's journey into the wilderness, and came and sat down under a juniper tree: and he requested for himself that he might die; and said, It is enough; now, O LORD, take away my life; for I am not better than my fathers
1 Kings 19:15	4057	And the LORD said unto him, Go, return on thy way to the wilderness of Damascus: and when thou comest, anoint Hazael to be king over Syria

2 Kings 3:8	4057	And he said, Which way shall we go up? And he answered, The way through the wilderness of Edom.
1 Chronicles 5:9	4057	And eastward he inhabited unto the entering in of the wilderness from the river Euphrates: because their cattle were multiplied in the land of Gilead
1 Chronicles 6:78	4057	And on the other side Jordan by Jericho, on the east side of Jordan, were given them out of the tribe of Reuben, Bezer in the wilderness with her suburbs, and Jahzah with her suburbs,
1 Chronicles 12:8	4057	For the tabernacle of the LORD, which Moses made in the wilderness, and the altar of the burnt offering, were at that season in the high place at Gibeon.
2 Chronicles 1:3	4057	So Solomon, and all the congregation with him, went to the high place that was at Gibeon; for there was the tabernacle of the congregation of God, which Moses the servant of the LORD had made in the wilderness
2 Chronicles 8:4	4057	And he built Tadmor in the wilderness, and all the store cities, which he built in Hamath
2 Chronicles 20:16	4057	To morrow go ye down against them: behold, they come up by the cliff of Ziz; and ye shall find them at the end of the brook, before the wilderness of Jeruel.
2 Chronicles 20:20	4057	And they rose early in the morning, and went forth into the wilderness of Tekoa: and as they went forth, Jehoshaphat stood and said, Hear me, O Judah, and ye inhabitants of Jerusalem; Believe in the LORD your God, so shall ye be established; believe his prophets, so shall ye prosper.
2 Chronicles 20:24	4057	And when Judah came toward the watch tower in the wilderness, they looked unto the multitude, and, behold, they were dead bodies fallen to the earth, and none escaped.
2 Chronicles 24:9	4057	And they made a proclamation through Judah and Jerusalem, to bring in to the LORD the collection that Moses the servant of God laid upon Israel in the wilderness.

Nehemiah 9:19	4057	Yet thou in thy manifold mercies forsookest them not in the wilderness: the pillar of the cloud departed not from them by day, to lead them in the way; neither the pillar of fire by night, to shew them light, and the way wherein they should go.
Nehemiah 9:21	4057	Yea, forty years didst thou sustain them in the wilderness, so that they lacked nothing; their clothes waxed not old, and their feet swelled not
Job 1:19	4057	And, behold, there came a great wind from the wilderness, and smote the four corners of the house, and it fell upon the young men, and they are dead; and I only am escaped alone to tell thee.
Job 12:24	8184	He taketh away the heart of the chief of the people of the earth, and causeth them to wander in a wilderness where there is no way.
Job 24:5	6160	Behold, as wild asses in the desert, go they forth to their work; rising betimes for a prey: the wilderness yieldeth food for them and for their children.
Job 30:3	6723	For want and famine they were solitary; fleeing into the wilderness in former time desolate and waste.
Job 38:26	4057	To cause it to rain on the earth, where no man is; on the wilderness, wherein there is no man;
Job 39:6	6160	Whose house I have made the wilderness, and the barren land his dwellings.
Psalms 29:8	4057	The voice of the LORD shaketh the wilderness; the LORD shaketh the wilderness of Kadesh
Psalms 55:7	4057	Lo, then would I wander far off, and remain in the wilderness. Selah
Psalms 63:t	4057	**A Psalm of David, when he was in the wilderness of Judah.** O God, thou art my God; early will I seek thee: my soul thirsteth for thee, my flesh longeth for thee in a dry and thirsty land, where no water is;
Psalms 65:12	4057	They drop upon the pastures of the wilderness: and the little hills rejoice on every side.

Psalms 68:7	3452	O God, when thou wentest forth before thy people, when thou didst march through the wilderness; Selah:
Psalms 72:9	6728	They that dwell in the wilderness shall bow before him; and his enemies shall lick the dust.
Psalms 74:14	6728	Thou brakest the heads of leviathan in pieces, and gavest him to be meat to the people inhabiting the wilderness.
Psalms 78:15	4057	He clave the rocks in the wilderness, and gave them drink as out of the great depths.
Psalms 78:17	6723	And they sinned yet more against him by provoking the most High in the wilderness.
Psalms 78:19	4057	Yea, they spake against God; they said, Can God furnish a table in the wilderness?
Psalms 78:40	4057	How oft did they provoke him in the wilderness, and grieve him in the desert!
Psalms 78:52	4057	But made his own people to go forth like sheep, and guided them in the wilderness like a flock.
Psalms 95:8	4057	Harden not your heart, as in the provocation, and as in the day of temptation in the wilderness:
Psalms 102:6	4057	I am like a pelican of the wilderness: I am like an owl of the desert.
Psalms 106:9	4057	He rebuked the Red sea also, and it was dried up: so he led them through the depths, as through the wilderness
Psalms 106:14	4057	But lusted exceedingly in the wilderness, and tempted God in the desert
Psalms 106:26	4057	Therefore he lifted up his hand against them, to overthrow them in the wilderness:
Psalms 107:4	4057	They wandered in the wilderness in a solitary way; they found no city to dwell in.
Psalms 107:33	4057	He turneth rivers into a wilderness, and the watersprings into dry ground;
Psalms 107:35	4057	He turneth the wilderness into a standing water, and dry ground into watersprings
Psalms 107:40	8414	He poureth contempt upon princes, and causeth them to wander in the wilderness, where there is no way.
Psalms 136:16	4057	To him which led his people through the wilderness: for his mercy endureth for ever
Proverbs 21:19	4057	It is better to dwell in the wilderness, than with a contentious and an angry woman

Song of Solomon 3:6	4057	Who is this that cometh out of the wilderness like pillars of smoke, perfumed with myrrh and frankincense, with all powders of the merchant?
Song of Solomon 8:5	4057	Who is this that cometh up from the wilderness, leaning upon her beloved? I raised thee up under the apple tree: there thy mother brought thee forth: there she brought thee forth that bare thee.
Isaiah 14:17	4057	That made the world as a wilderness, and destroyed the cities thereof; that opened not the house of his prisoners?
Isaiah 16:1	4057	Send ye the lamb to the ruler of the land from Sela to the wilderness, unto the mount of the daughter of Zion.
Isaiah 16:8	4057	For the fields of Heshbon languish, and the vine of Sibmah: the lords of the heathen have broken down the principal plants thereof, they are come even unto Jazer, they wandered through the wilderness: her branches are stretched out, they are gone over the sea.
Isaiah 23:13	6728	Behold the land of the Chaldeans; this people was not, till the Assyrian founded it for them that dwell in the wilderness: they set up the towers thereof, they raised up the palaces thereof; and he brought it to ruin.
Isaiah 27:10	4057	Yet the defenced city shall be desolate, and the habitation forsaken, and left like a wilderness: there shall the calf feed, and there shall he lie down, and consume the branches thereof.
Isaiah 32:15-16	4057	Until the spirit be poured upon us from on high, and the wilderness be a fruitful field, and the fruitful field be counted for a forest. Then judgment shall dwell in the wilderness, and righteousness remain in the fruitful field.
Isaiah 33:9	6160	The earth mourneth and languisheth: Lebanon is ashamed and hewn down: Sharon is like a wilderness; and Bashan and Carmel shake off their fruits.
Isaiah 35:1	4057	The wilderness and the solitary place shall be glad for them; and the desert shall rejoice, and blossom as the rose

Isaiah 40:3	4057	The voice of him that crieth in the wilderness, Prepare ye the way of the LORD, make straight in the desert a highway for our God
Isaiah 41:18-19	4057	I will open rivers in high places, and fountains in the midst of the valleys: I will make the wilderness a pool of water, and the dry land springs of water. I will plant in the wilderness the cedar, the shittah tree, and the myrtle, and the oil tree; I will set in the desert the fir tree, and the pine, and the box tree together:
Isaiah 42:11	4057	Let the wilderness and the cities thereof lift up their voice, the villages that Kedar doth inhabit: let the inhabitants of the rock sing, let them shout from the top of the mountains.
Isaiah 43:19-20	4057	Behold, I will do a new thing; now it shall spring forth; shall ye not know it? I will even make a way in the wilderness, and rivers in the desert. The beast of the field shall honour me, the dragons and the owls: because I give waters in the wilderness, and rivers in the desert, to give drink to my people, my chosen.
Isaiah 50:2	4057	Wherefore, when I came, was there no man? when I called, was there none to answer? Is my hand shortened at all, that it cannot redeem? or have I no power to deliver? behold, at my rebuke I dry up the sea, I make the rivers a wilderness: their fish stinketh, because there is no water, and dieth for thirst.
Isaiah 51:3	4057	For the LORD shall comfort Zion: he will comfort all her waste places; and he will make her wilderness like Eden, and her desert like the garden of the LORD; joy and gladness shall be found therein, thanksgiving, and the voice of melody.
Isaiah 63:13	4057	That led them through the deep, as an horse in the wilderness, that they should not stumble?
Isaiah 64:10	4057	Thy holy cities are a wilderness, Zion is a wilderness, Jerusalem a desolation.
Jeremiah 2:2	4057	Go and cry in the ears of Jerusalem, saying, Thus saith the LORD; I remember thee, the kindness of thy youth, the love of thine espousals, when thou wentest after me in the wilderness, in a land that was not sown.

Jeremiah 2:6	4057	Neither said they, Where is the LORD that brought us up out of the land of Egypt, that led us through the wilderness, through a land of deserts and of pits, through a land of drought, and of the shadow of death, through a land that no man passed through, and where no man dwelt?
Jeremiah 2:24	4057	A wild ass used to the wilderness, that snuffeth up the wind at her pleasure; in her occasion who can turn her away? all they that seek her will not weary themselves; in her month they shall find her.
Jeremiah 2 :31	4057	O generation, see ye the word of the LORD. Have I been a wilderness unto Israel? a land of darkness? wherefore say my people, We are lords; we will come no more unto thee?
Jeremiah 3:2	4057	Lift up thine eyes unto the high places, and see where thou hast not been lien with. In the ways hast thou sat for them, as the Arabian in the wilderness; and thou hast polluted the land with
Jeremiah 4:11	4057	At that time shall it be said to this people and to Jerusalem, A dry wind of the high places in the wilderness toward the daughter of my people, not to fan, nor to cleanse,
Jeremiah 4:26	4057	I beheld, and, lo, the fruitful place was a wilderness, and all the cities thereof were broken down at the presence of the LORD, and by his fierce anger.
Jeremiah 9:2	4057	Oh that I had in the wilderness a lodging place of wayfaring men; that I might leave my people, and go from them! for they be all adulterers, an assembly of treacherous men.
Jeremiah 9:10	4057	For the mountains will I take up a weeping and wailing, and for the habitations of the wilderness a lamentation, because they are burned up, so that none can pass through them; neither can men hear the voice of the cattle; both the fowl of the heavens and the beast are fled; they are gone.

Jeremiah 9:12	4057	Who is the wise man, that may understand this? and who is he to whom the mouth of the LORD hath spoken, that he may declare it, for what the land perisheth and is burned up like a wilderness, that none passeth through?
Jeremiah 9:26	4057	Egypt, and Judah, and Edom, and the children of Ammon, and Moab, and all that are in the utmost corners, that dwell in the wilderness: for all these nations are uncircumcised, and all the house of Israel are uncircumcised in the heart.
Jeremiah 12:10	4057	Many pastors have destroyed my vineyard, they have trodden my portion under foot, they have made my pleasant portion a desolate wilderness.
Jeremiah 12:12	4057	The spoilers are come upon all high places through the wilderness: for the sword of the LORD shall devour from the one end of the land even to the other end of the land: no flesh shall have peace.
Jeremiah 13:24	4057	Therefore will I scatter them as the stubble that passeth away by the wind of the wilderness.
Jeremiah 17:6	4057	For he shall be like the heath in the desert, and shall not see when good cometh; but shall inhabit the parched places in the wilderness, in a salt land and not inhabited.
Jeremiah 22:6	4057	For thus saith the LORD unto the king's house of Judah; Thou art Gilead unto me, and the head of Lebanon: yet surely I will make thee a wilderness, and cities which are not inhabited.
Jeremiah 23:10	4057	For the land is full of adulterers; for because of swearing the land mourneth; the pleasant places of the wilderness are dried up, and their course is evil, and their force is not right
Jeremiah 31:2	4057	Thus saith the LORD, The people which were left of the sword found grace in the wilderness; even Israel, when I went to cause him to rest.
Jeremiah 48:6	4057	Flee, save your lives, and be like the heath in the wilderness.
Jeremiah 50:12	4057	Your mother shall be sore confounded; she that bare you shall be ashamed: behold, the hindermost of the nations shall be a wilderness, a dry land, and a desert.

Jeremiah 51:43	4057	Her cities are a desolation, a dry land, and a wilderness, a land wherein no man dwelleth, neither doth any son of man pass thereby.
Lamentations 4:3	4057	Even the sea monsters draw out the breast, they give suck to their young ones: the daughter of my people is become cruel, like the ostriches in the wilderness.
Lamentations 4:19	4057	Our persecutors are swifter than the eagles of the heaven: they pursued us upon the mountains, they laid wait for us in the wilderness.
Lamentations 5:9	4057	We gat our bread with the peril of our lives because of the sword of the wilderness
Ezekiel 6:14	4057	So will I stretch out my hand upon them, and make the land desolate, yea, more desolate than the wilderness toward Diblath, in all their habitations: and they shall know that I am the LORD.
Ezekiel 19:13	4057	And now she is planted in the wilderness, in a dry and thirsty ground.
Ezekiel 20:10	4057	Wherefore I caused them to go forth out of the land of Egypt, and brought them into the wilderness
Ezekiel 20:13	4057	But the house of Israel rebelled against me in the wilderness: they walked not in my statutes, and they despised my judgments, which if a man do, he shall even live in them; and my sabbaths they greatly polluted: then I said, I would pour out my fury upon them in the wilderness, to consume them.
Ezekiel 20:15	4057	Yet also I lifted up my hand unto them in the wilderness, that I would not bring them into the land which I had given them, flowing with milk and honey, which is the glory of all lands;
Ezekiel 20:17-18	4057	Nevertheless mine eye spared them from destroying them, neither did I make an end of them in the wilderness. But I said unto their children in the wilderness, Walk ye not in the statutes of your fathers, neither observe their judgments, nor defile yourselves with their

Ezekiel 20:21	4057	Notwithstanding the children rebelled against me: they walked not in my statutes, neither kept my judgments to do them, which if a man do, he shall even live in them; they polluted my sabbaths: then I said, I would pour out my fury upon them, to accomplish my anger against them in the wilderness.
Ezekiel 20:23	4057	I lifted up mine hand unto them also in the wilderness, that I would scatter them among the heathen, and disperse them through the countries;
Ezekiel 20:35-36	4057	And I will bring you into the wilderness of the people, and there will I plead with you face to face. Like as I pleaded with your fathers in the wilderness of the land of Egypt, so will I plead with you, saith the Lord GOD
Ezekiel 23:42	4057	And a voice of a multitude being at ease was with her: and with the men of the common sort were brought Sabeans from the wilderness, which put bracelets upon their hands, and beautiful crowns
Ezekiel 29:5	4057	And I will leave thee thrown into the wilderness, thee and all the fish of thy rivers: thou shalt fall upon the open fields; thou shalt not be brought together, nor gathered: I have given thee for meat to the beasts of the field and to the fowls of the heaven
Ezekiel 34:25	4057	And I will make with them a covenant of peace, and will cause the evil beasts to cease out of the land: and they shall dwell safely in the wilderness, and sleep in the woods.
Hosea 2:3	4057	Lest I strip her naked, and set her as in the day that she was born, and make her as a wilderness, and set her like a dry land, and slay her with thirst.
Hosea 2:14	4057	Therefore, behold, I will allure her, and bring her into the wilderness, and speak comfortably unto her.
Hosea 9:10	4057	I found Israel like grapes in the wilderness; I saw your fathers as the firstripe in the fig tree at her first time: but they went to Baalpeor, and separated themselves unto that shame; and their abominations were according as they loved.

Hosea 13:5	4057	I did know thee in the wilderness, in the land of great drought.
Joel 1:19-20	4057	O LORD, to thee will I cry: for the fire hath devoured the pastures of the wilderness, and the flame hath burned all the trees of the field. The beasts of the field cry also unto thee: for the rivers of waters are dried up, and the fire hath devoured the pastures of the wilderness.
Joel 2:3	4057	A fire devoureth before them; and behind them a flame burneth: the land is as the garden of Eden before them, and behind them a desolate wilderness; yea, and nothing shall escape them.
Joel 2:22	4057	Be not afraid, ye beasts of the field: for the pastures of the wilderness do spring, for the tree beareth her fruit, the fig tree and the vine do yield their strength.
Joel 3:19	4057	Egypt shall be a desolation, and Edom shall be a desolate wilderness, for the violence against the children of Judah, because they have shed innocent blood in their land.
Amos 2:10	4057	Also I brought you up from the land of Egypt, and led you forty years through the wilderness, to possess the land of the Amorite.
Amos 5:25	4057	Have ye offered unto me sacrifices and offerings in the wilderness forty years, O house of Israel?
Amos 6:14	6166	But, behold, I will raise up against you a nation, O house of Israel, saith the LORD the God of hosts; and they shall afflict you from the entering in of Hemath unto the river of the wilderness.
Zephaniah 2:13	4057	And he will stretch out his hand against the north, and destroy Assyria; and will make Nineveh a desolation, and dry like a wilderness.
Malachi 1:3	4057	And I hated Esau, and laid his mountains and his heritage waste for the dragons of the wilderness
Matthew 3:1	2048	In those days came John the Baptist, preaching in the wilderness of Judaea,

Matthew 3:3	2048	For this is he that was spoken of by the prophet Esaias, saying, The voice of one crying in the wilderness, Prepare ye the way of the Lord, make his paths straight.
Matthew 4:1	2048	Then was Jesus led up of the Spirit into the wilderness to be tempted of the devil.
Matthew 11:7	2048	And as they departed, Jesus began to say unto the multitudes concerning John, What went ye out into the wilderness to see? A reed shaken with the wind?
Matthew 15:33	2047	And his disciples say unto him, Whence should we have so much bread in the wilderness, as to fill so great a multitude?
Mark 1:3-4	2048	The voice of one crying in the wilderness, Prepare ye the way of the Lord, make his paths straight. John did baptize in the wilderness, and preach the baptism of repentance for the remission of sins.
Mark 1:12-13	2048	And immediately the Spirit driveth him into the wilderness. And he was there in the wilderness forty days, tempted of Satan; and was with the wild beasts; and the angels ministered unto him.
Mark 8:24	2047	And his disciples answered him, From whence can a man satisfy these men with bread here in the wilderness?
Luke 3:2	2048	Annas and Caiaphas being the high priests, the word of God came unto John the son of Zacharias in the wilderness
Luke 3:4	2048	As it is written in the book of the words of Esaias the prophet, saying, The voice of one crying in the wilderness, Prepare ye the way of the Lord, make his paths straight
Luke 5:16	2048	And he withdrew himself into the wilderness, and prayed.
Luke 7:24	2048	And when the messengers of John were departed, he began to speak unto the people concerning John, What went ye out into the wilderness for to see? A reed shaken with the wind?

Luke 8:29	2048	(For he had commanded the unclean spirit to come out of the man. For oftentimes it had caught him: and he was kept bound with chains and in fetters; and he brake the bands, and was driven of the devil into the wilderness.)
Luke 15:4	2048	What man of you, having an hundred sheep, if he lose one of them, doth not leave the ninety and nine in the wilderness, and go after that which is lost, until he find it?
John 1:23	2048	He said, I am the voice of one crying in the wilderness, Make straight the way of the Lord, as said the prophet Esaias
John 3:14	2048	But whosoever drinketh of the water that I shall give him shall never thirst; but the water that I shall give him shall be in him a well of water springing up into everlasting life.
John 6:49	2048	Your fathers did eat manna in the wilderness, and are dead.
John 11:54	2048	Jesus therefore walked no more openly among the Jews; but went thence unto a country near to the wilderness, into a city called Ephraim, and there continued with his disciples.
Acts 7:30	2048	And when forty years were expired, there appeared to him in the wilderness of mount Sina an angel of the Lord in a flame of fire in a bush
Acts 7:37-38	2048	This is that Moses, which said unto the children of Israel, A prophet shall the Lord your God raise up unto you of your brethren, like unto me; him shall ye hear. This is he, that was in the church in the wilderness with the angel which spake to him in the mount Sina, and with our fathers: who received the lively oracles to give unto us:
Acts 7:42	2048	Then God turned, and gave them up to worship the host of heaven; as it is written in the book of the prophets, O ye house of Israel, have ye offered to me slain beasts and sacrifices by the space of forty years in the wilderness?

Acts 7:44	2048	Our fathers had the tabernacle of witness in the wilderness, as he had appointed, speaking unto Moses, that he should make it according to the fashion that he had seen. But with many of them God was not well pleased: for they were overthrown in the wilderness.
Acts 13:18	2048	And about the time of forty years suffered he their manners in the wilderness.
Acts 21:38	2048	Art not thou that Egyptian, which before these days madest an uproar, and leddest out into the wilderness four thousand men that were murderers?
1 Corinthians 10:5	2048	But with many of them God was not well pleased: for they were overthrown in the wilderness.
2 Corinthians 11:26	2047	For as often as ye eat this bread, and drink this cup, ye do shew the Lord's death till he come.
Hebrews 3:8	2048	Harden not your hearts, as in the provocation, in the day of temptation in the wilderness:
Hebrews 3:17	2048	But with whom was he grieved forty years? was it not with them that had sinned, whose carcases fell in the wilderness?
Revelation 12:6	2048	And the woman fled into the wilderness, where she hath a place prepared of God, that they should feed her there a thousand two hundred and threescore days.
Revelation 12:14	2048	And to the woman were given two wings of a great eagle, that she might fly into the wilderness, into her place, where she is nourished for a time, and times, and half a time, from the face of the serpent.
Revelation 17:3	2048	So he carried me away in the spirit into the wilderness: and I saw a woman sit upon a scarlet coloured beast, full of names of blasphemy, having seven heads and ten horns.

Bibliography

Youngblood, Ronald F; Bruce, E.F; Harrison, R.K. *"Compact Bible Dictionary"* Nashville; Thomas Nelson Publishers, 2004

Nave, O.J. *"Nave's Topical Bible"* Nashville: Thomas Nelson Inc., Publishers, 1979.

Vine, W.E., *"Vine's Expository Dictionary of Old & New Testament Words"*, Nashville: Thomas Nelson Publishers, 1997.

Zodhiates, S. Th.D., Baker, W.D.R.E., *"Hebrew-Greek Key Word Study Bible King James Version"*, Chattanooga: AMG Publishers, 1991.

Hawkins, J.M., *"The St. Michael Oxford Dictionary"*, London, Artus: Publishing Company Limited 1981.

Bailey, M., Constable, T.; Swindoll, C.R; Zuck, R.B; *"Nelson's New Testament Survey"*, Nashville: Word Publishing, 1999.

Dyer, C; Mserrill, E.; Swindoll, C. R., Zuck, R.B., *"Nelson's Old Testament Survey"*, Nashville: Word Publishing, 2001.

Radmacker, E.D. Th.D.; Allen, R.B. Th.D.; House, H.W. Th.D.;J.D.; *"The Nelson Study Bible New King James Version"*, Nashville: Thomas Nelson Publishers, 1997

Strong, J. LL.D., S.T.D.; *"The New Strong's Exhaustive Concordance of the Bible"*, Nashville: Thomas Nelson Inc., 1990.

Adaptation *"Rebirth of the Eagle"* by Mike-ruppi_scifi@yahoo.de

Websites:

http://virtualreligion.net/iho/herod2.html
http://www.egyptiangods.co.uk/statutes.htm
http://biblelight.net/moses.htm
http://gwydir.demon.co.uk/jo/egypt/index.htm
http://en.wikipedia.org/wiki/Herod_Antipas

Commentaries

E-Sword Bible Study Commentary - Gill
E- Sword Bible Study Commentary - Clarke

Endnotes

The Nelson's Study Bible – NKJV

1 Samuel 17:4 records Goliath's height as six cubits and a span.

A cubit = 18 inches a span = 9 inches

F.F. Bruce, *"Herod Antipas, Tetrarch of Galilee and Peraea", The Annual of Leeds University Oriental Society* 5 (1963/65): 6-23

About the Author

 Dr Claudette King is an author, bible teacher and seminar speaker. She operates an online bible college which allows learners to gain insight into theological revelations from the convenience of their home, anywhere in the world. With an internet connection, students can access the bible college and begin their theological journey. Visit www.iaulondon.co.uk for more details.

Find out more about Dr King from her website, visit her today at www.drclaudetteking.com

Gender*less* Anointing
There is neither male nor female
ISBN 978-0-9570463-1-3 (Paperback)
ISBN 978-0-9570463-0-6 (Hardback)

This book takes the reader through the corridors of time introducing the societal and hierarchical status placed on women within the several social classes. An eye-opening investigation into the social customs, beliefs and practices encouraging Paul's writing. Spanning the bronze age and into the twenty-first century; its reader is provided with answers to aged-old questions regarding the writings of Paul and the supposed silence of women.

ORDER IN THE CHURCH SEMINAR
"Let all things be done decently and in order" (1 Corinthians 14:40)

Whether you are a church leader, auxiliary head, minister, aspiring leader, church administrator, trustee or youth leader, this is for you.

'Order in the Church' is a thought-provoking seminar dealing with Administrative, Governmental, Ministerial and Spiritual Order.

Dr Claudette King is available to conduct this seminar at your assembly.

ORDER IN THE CHURCH DVD & WORKBOOK
"Let all things be done decently and in order" (1 Corinthians 14:40)

Want to hear the seminar but not able to have Dr King come to you, then why not purchase the DVD and workbook today?

  The DVD is of an actual session taught with the accompanying workbook, you will feel you are in the session. Complete your workbook, pause and rewind and repeat as many times as you desire to grasp clearer understanding on any of the areas taught.

Not sure what to expect, you can view a video clip of what people thought of the seminar. To view the video and find out more about the seminar, visit her website www.drclaudettking.com. All products are available from her website.

COMING SOON!!! 'ORDER IN THE CHURCH' THE BOOK
Scheduled to be released 2012

IAU LONDON
The fully online theological Seminary

Want to know more the word of God? Would like to study but don't feel you have the time? Have many questions and want to do a Bible course or even study to degree level?

IAU London allows you to gleam more from the word of God, at your pace, from the convenience of your home and at a level you desire. Armed with a computer/laptop and an internet connection, you can become a student with IAU London. An online campus that allows you to meet other students, liaise with available lecturers, and access archived as well as live classes. For more details visit us online www.iaulondon.co.uk

11202076R00137

Made in the USA
Charleston, SC
06 February 2012